The Bird Watcher's Bible

The Bird Watcher's Bible

George Laycock

Second Edition
Revised and Updated

DOUBLEDAY
NEW YORK   LONDON   TORONTO   SYDNEY   AUCKLAND

PUBLISHED BY DOUBLEDAY
a division of Bantam Doubleday Dell Publishing Group, Inc.
1540 Broadway, New York, New York 10036

DOUBLEDAY and the portrayal of an anchor with a dolphin
are registered trademarks of Doubleday, a division of Bantam
Doubleday Dell Publishing Group, Inc.

Library of Congress Cataloging-in-Publication Data

Laycock, George.
    The bird watcher's bible / George Laycock.—[Rev. ed.]
        p.   cm.
    ISBN 0-385-46835-0
    1. Bird watching—United States.   2. Bird attracting—
        United States.   3. Birds—United States.
    I. Title.
    QL682.L39   1994
    598'.0723473 -- dc20   93-32541
                                                CIP

February 1994

10   9   8   7   6   5   4   3   2   1

Contents

Part III   Some Common Birds

Part IV   Equipment for Bird Watchers

Part V   Attracting Birds

Part VI   Where to See Birds

Acknowledgments

For their generous help during the preparation of this book I wish to extend my thanks to the birders, ornithologists, and skilled wildlife photographers who helped me gather information and illustrations. Special thanks are due Karl H. Maslowski, DeVere Burt, Don Cook, Carrol Henderson, and Luther C. Goldman for their contributions to the illustrations.

A note of sincere appreciation is also due those who read the manuscript critically before publication and whose suggestions were beneficial in bringing the book to its final form.

Serious bird watchers in every state were instrumental in helping me to compile the section on the best bird-watching areas. I extend my thanks to each of them for suggestions and for checking the final copy for each state.

I

BIRDS AND BIRD WATCHERS

Crow-sized pileated woodpecker, about to feed its hungry young, has increased in recent times and is often seen in wooded areas within city limits. *Karl H. Maslowski.*

Birds and People

Deep in the forests of Michigan, two burly loggers, rushing ahead with their heavy work, knocked over the decaying stump of an old birch tree. Ordinarily this was nothing to be concerned about. But on this occasion half a dozen baby chickadees fluttered helplessly to the ground around the loggers' boots. Left alone, the baby birds would have died in a matter of hours. Now the loggers had a problem. Work stopped. Tools were laid aside, and the little birds were quickly gathered up and put in a hat.

Then the loggers set the hollow log back on its stump and, using splints and rope, bound it to its base again. Tenderly they put the little chickadees back into their nest, then withdrew to the shadows of some nearby bushes to see what would happen. The parent birds soon returned, carrying food for their chicks. The repair job was perfectly acceptable to them. They delivered the food to their young and flew off for more as if nothing had happened. The loggers, feeling much relieved, went back to their work.

Elsewhere people in all walks of life have their own experiences with birds. For many it is enough to watch them from the kitchen window.

Nobody knows how many bird watchers there are today. One estimate places the figure in excess of eighty million. We spend millions of dollars every year buying feed to attract birds to our yards.

There are several reasons for the popularity of bird watching. Birds are highly visible. They are around us all year, playing roles in an outdoor drama that changes players with the seasons. Winter brings feathered visitors down from faraway northern places. Spring promises the return of others after long and mysterious journeys to distant southern wintering grounds.

But perhaps the greatest appeal of all in bird watching is that anyone can get in on the fun: man, woman, or child, young or old, healthy or infirm. There is no need for great skills or knowledge in the beginning. But neither is there a limit to what one may discover in studying these feathered neighbors. Wherever the bird watcher travels around the world, he can compare the birds of foreign lands—700 species in Australia, 250 in the British Isles, or 450 in Western Europe—with those of his home neighborhood, and add new birds to his continually growing list.

Bird watching is a bonus, an added reward that goes with many kinds of other outdoor adventures. Fishermen and hunters frequently stop in their tracks to watch some unfamiliar bird fly out of sight. Hikers take note of the birds along their trails. Campers want to know the birds outside their tents or in the countryside to which their trailers, boats, and motor homes transport them.

At home, all who work in their gardens or watch over their lawns become, at some time, bird watchers. Often their curiosity about birds leads to the purchase of binoculars and bird guides, and whole new worlds open for them.

Birders Aid Science

Amateur bird watchers have made numerous dramatic and important scientific discoveries by studying the birds around them. One of these was Charles L. Broley, who managed a bank in Winnipeg, Manitoba. With his wife he went out into the wet prairies and along the ponds and rivers at every opportunity to check the recent arrivals. He kept track of the migrating waterfowl and knew when the shorebirds passed through on their annual travels to and from their northern nesting territories.

Then came the time for Broley to retire. He and his wife planned to go to Florida, where they had been spending winter vacations for several years. Once there, Broley would sit in the sun. He would, of course, continue his bird watching, but he did not plan any bird watching that would be particularly demanding.

On that trip south, however, he stopped off in Washington, D.C., for a visit with his friend Richard H. Pough, a professional ornithologist and conservationist employed by the National Audubon Society. Pough gave him a few bands of the right size to fit the leg of a bald eagle and

Semipalmated sandpiper is one of the common shorebirds often spotted on sandbars and mud flats around both fresh- and saltwater.

Brown pelican is often seen along the seashores where it fishes for a living and stops to rest on a convenient piling.

suggested that, once in Florida, Broley might place the bands on eagles about to leave the nest for the first time.

For a man in his sixties this seemed a considerable assignment. Florida's bald eagles customarily nest in the very tops of the tallest pine trees. But Broley thought about eagle banding considerably as he drove southward. The fact that anyone ascending to eagle nests would have to be a vigorous and daring climber did not strike Broley as much of a barrier. He was a small and nimble man in good physical condition and he kept himself fit by his daily exercise.

He soon invented a system of ropes and rope

ladders and found that he could scale the trees in which the eagles lived. That summer he placed official leg bands on a number of eaglets and in following summers increased his eagle-banding efforts. By the time he died, not by falling from an eagle nest tree, but while fighting a brush fire, he had banded over twelve hundred bald eagles, more than had ever been banded before. From this amateur's eagle studies, scientists understood for the first time the strange migration patterns sometimes made by young bald eagles of Florida. Broley, because of his banding, was also one of the first to learn that the national bird was in trouble. In his first years of eagle banding he located as many as 125 nests a year and clamped the official aluminum bands to the legs of about 150 young eagles annually. This was exciting business for Broley. He was happy in the volunteer work he was doing for the national bird. Then, suddenly, he was finding fewer young eagles in the nests, while many nests produced no young at all. Finally, there came a year when Broley found only one young eagle to band. He made no pretense of being a scientist, but he was a keen observer, and he became one of the first people to say, correctly, that such pesticides as DDT might be causing the disappearance of the bald eagle.

Another amateur turned professional was Margaret Morse Nice, the wife of a professor and mother of four daughters, who began feeding birds in her Columbus, Ohio, backyard for the same reasons anyone feeds them. But Mrs. Nice saw more than some of us might. She was a close observer of the birds in her yard, and eventually she began in-depth studies of song sparrows. She studied their actions toward one another and made notes on what she saw. She talked with professional naturalists, some of whom told her that everything was already known about song sparrows. Mrs. Nice eventually proved, however, that very little had been learned about these birds. Her observations went into a book on song-sparrow behavior, *Studies in the Life History of the Song Sparrow.** It became a classic among bird books and still stands as a model for scientists writing life-history studies of wild species.

Another amateur bird watcher whose work will long be remembered is Harold Mayfield, of Toledo, Ohio. Much of his time in the field was spent in the company of Josselyn Van Tyne, curator of birds at the University of Michigan's Museum of Zoology. Van Tyne and Mayfield were particularly interested in a flashy yellow and gray warbler first discovered by another

amateur naturalist, Dr. Jared P. Kirtland, a Cleveland, Ohio, physician.

Today it is known as Kirtland's warbler, and its scientific name is *Dendroica kirtlandii.* But from the beginning there were deep mysteries surrounding its life. It was found to winter in the Bahamas, and as to where it might go to rear its young, the ornithologists could only guess. Eventually it was discovered nesting in the jack pine forests of Michigan. All the world's Kirtland's warblers nested there, within an area covering only a few Michigan counties.

In addition, it demanded highly specialized nesting conditions. It built its nest in the grasses and weeds at the base of jack pine trees, but only where there are jack pines between six and eighteen feet high. These are young pine forests, and the jack pine only grows where there has been fire to open the tough cones of the pines so the seeds will germinate. The Kirtland's warbler, as the ornithologists began to understand, could only live where fire had burned the woods. Today the U.S. Forest Service, working in that part of Michigan, prepares new areas for the scarce Kirtland's warbler by setting fire to the old forest. It was in these managed jack pine forests that I first added the Kirtland's warbler to my bird list some years ago. Once in their territories, they are easily seen. During the summer months the males sing in loud, clear tones from the dead tips of the tallest jack pines in their territories.

Josselyn Van Tyne died before he could complete his Kirtland's warbler studies. Harold Mayfield, the bird watcher from Toledo, took over. He had learned so much about this demanding little bird that he wrote the book Van Tyne had once begun on the life of Kirtland's warbler, and it can be found today in science libraries wherever ornithologists study.

Still another amateur bird watcher whose observations gained him fame among scientists was H. Elliot Howard, an English businessman. He discovered, by watching them, that mated

---

* New York: Dover Publications, 1964. 2 vols.

birds in spring and summer have regular singing posts to which they return time and again. Singing is not just a random, exuberant bubbling over of spirit by a male bird seeking to attract female attention, and Howard was perhaps the first to learn it. Some birds sing to mark their territories and guard them against others of their kind. In 1920 Howard published his first book, *Territory in Bird Life,* and it became a classic in its field. Today Howard is remembered, not for his work in industry, but for his five bird books and his quiet probing into the hidden secrets of the outdoors.

During more than fifty years of writing his weekly column "Naturalist Afield," in the Cincinnati, Ohio, *Enquirer,* Karl H. Maslowski came to expect unusual, and often exciting, reports from amateur bird watchers. A housewife called him one winter day at his office to report that she had a green-tailed towhee visiting her bird feeder. Maslowski, a long-time nature photographer and Audubon Society lecturer, explained to the lady that the green-tailed towhee belongs in the dry lands of the Southwest and that there had never been one reported anywhere in Ohio. But she was so persistent that he drove out to the home. There, to his astonishment, was a green-tailed towhee more than fifteen hundred miles from where it would be expected to be. Maslowski promptly photographed it, and, thanks to the alert amateur, a new species was added to the list of Ohio birds.

Another reader saw a strange junco at his feeder, checked it out in his bird guide, then called Maslowski. Again the naturalist went out to investigate and promptly verified the report of the only gray-headed junco ever recorded in the state. He also recalls the reader who reported a black-headed grosbeak, normally found only west of the Mississippi. Again the reader's identification was correct, and a new bird was added to Ohio's list, helping to prove once more that anyone, if interested enough, may make important discoveries in the bird world.

But the strangest of all such reports coming to Maslowski over the years was a reader's account of the unusual bird nest in the shrubbery outside his door. The reader said that a pair of robins and a pair of cardinals were sharing a nest. This report also proved to be true. Crowded into the single nest were both young robins and young cardinals while the mixed parents shared the feeding chores—perhaps the only case of its kind ever reported.

How Many Birds?

During the summer of 1973 a strange and exciting event occurred far up on the forested slopes of Haleakala on the Hawaiian island of Maui. Student ornithologists camped there discovered a sparrow-sized bird they did not recognize. No one recognized it and for a good reason: It had never before been recorded by man. This remarkable discovery of a new Hawaiian honeycreeper caused

Barn owls are birds of the night. These five youngsters have flourished on the diet of rats and mice delivered by their parents.

a wave of excitement through the world of ornithology. Most of the world's birds have almost certainly now been duly discovered and described.

Around the world they number about 9,000 species. They are most numerous and varied in the tropics, with the variety diminishing and the numbers dwindling toward the cold regions of the poles. For all of North America there are about 1,780 species listed, and for the continent north of Mexico about 800 species, counting not only the nesting birds but also wanderers.

Birds vary greatly in their range of sizes. The biggest of all living forms are the flightless ostriches, which may weigh more than three hundred pounds. Not many hundreds of years ago even larger birds existed. The elephant birds that lived on Madagascar are believed to have weighed as much as a thousand pounds, and their egg shells were used by native people as jugs that held two gallons of liquid. At the other end of the scale are the tiny hummingbirds, which flit like large hawk moths among the flowers. Smallest of all is the bee hummingbird of Cuba, a sprite that is only two and a half inches long, bill included, and so light that four hundred birds would weigh only a pound.

Between these extremes are birds of all sizes, adapted to fit the living conditions of nearly every corner of the world.

A majority of the world's birds, more than

Clark's nutcracker, known by its black wings and gray body, is a common visitor around campsites in western coniferous forests.

Common raven is known for its intelligence. It is a wilderness bird, but sometimes adapts to life around towns.

American coot is a common waterbird over much of North America.

Anhinga, which lives on freshwater fish, is often seen perched as it dries its outstretched wings.

Favorite of seaside birders is the brown pelican, which flies in formation and wades in shallow waters.

5,000 of the 9,000 species, are included in the order Passeriformes, the perching birds. Among these are most of the birds likely to come to our winter feeders or nest around our homes and gardens, including such birds as the finches, warblers, thrushes, chickadees, and titmice.

Wherever we see birds, however, we might marvel at their uniformity, in spite of their variation in size and shape. Among mammals are species that travel on two feet, four feet, or flippers. Some, such as whales and dolphins, live in the ocean, never coming to land. Bats are mammals that spend much of their time flying. Reptiles also come in wide variety, including some that have feet and others that have none. But birds, every one of them, are equipped with two feet and a covering of feathers. Besides, they possess other features that set them apart.

How Birds Are Equipped

Every part of the bird seems especially adapted. Consider the bird's bill and what might be viewed as a strange shape for an animal's mouth. The head of the bird, like the rest of it, is light in weight for its size. Skull bones are thin. Teeth, once prominent equipment in the reptilian ancestors of birds 150 million years ago, have been sacrificed. The bills of birds, tough and lightweight, are marvels of adaptation, a principle tool aiding the bird in its constant struggle for survival. The long slender bills of the brown creeper or the nuthatch allow them to reach into narrow crevices where insects are hidden. The short, stout bills of the finches are well suited to gathering and crushing seeds. The long stilettolike bills of the herons are precisely what these wading birds need for capturing the fish on which they live. The heavy curved bill of the hawk is a meat hook for tearing its food into bite size. The long slender bill of the woodcock is a perfect pair of tweezers for probing deep into the moist earth and lift-

Black-necked stilt finds its food while wading on long legs in shallow water.

Our national bird, the bald eagle, uses its hooked beak for tearing food apart.

ing nutritious earthworms from their holes. The pelican comes equipped with a long bill that has a built-in fish scoop.

Those large eyes with which birds have evolved provide them with a gift of vision superior to that of all other vertebrates, including man. The soaring hawk, for example, sees its prey in far greater detail than a man would from the same distance. The image is sharper, about eight times sharper, for the hawk than for man, and this, plus a binocular vision that aids in judging distances, gives the hunting bird an advantage in its search for food.

The owl has highly sensitive ears. Furthermore, the ears are not aligned in the skull. Instead, one ear is slightly lower on the head than the other is, and this enables the owl to pinpoint the location of prey by triangulation alone. Tests have proved that barn owls can catch mice with uncanny accuracy in total darkness.

The feet of birds have adapted to fit them for special life styles. Some form a lock-grip on limbs, permitting perching birds to sleep without falling off. Others, broad and webbed, become paddles for birds that spend much of their time swimming. Feet of predatory birds are used for capturing and killing prey. The coot has lobed feet useful for both swimming and walking on mud.

Most of all, however, consider the marvel of the feather, a strong, lightweight structure with a hollow shaft with barbs and barbules that overlap and often interlock. Properly cared for, the feathers become protection against the elements, and those of the tail and wings particularly help to make flight possible. In addition, these are replaceable parts, and the wing pri-

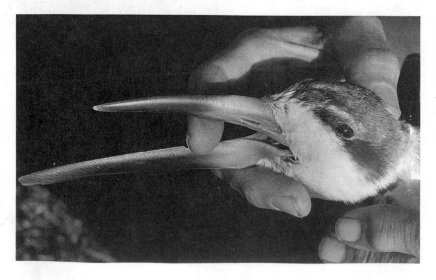

Black skimmer is a coastal bird that has a longer lower mandible with which it cuts through the water surface when pursuing small fish. This skimmer was captured for banding.

maries or other feathers, sometimes worn and tattered, will be replaced by new ones, for all birds undergo a molt at least once a year.

Feathers help to make flight possible, and flight has lifted the birds of the world to a status in the realm of animals that gives them special advantages in finding food and escaping enemies. This ability to take to the wing had its origin, perhaps, with small climbing reptiles that first leaped, then eventually glided from limb to limb, or limb to ground. This began perhaps 150 million years ago. Gradually front legs became wings, and it is believed that the scales that formed the outer covering changed, adapted, and continued to change until some of them became feathers. Not all of them have changed even to this day; the legs of birds are still covered with scales. Meanwhile, bones became hollow and lighter in weight, and breast muscles increased in size and strength to propel the wings.

With the passage of time and millions of years of adaptive radiation, birds evolved to fit

The graceful flight of the gull is an excellent subject for photographers.

Ruffed grouse, such as this male bird on his drumming log during courtship season, is a forest dweller. *Wisconsin Department of Natural Resources.*

into every niche until today they live from Arctic to Antarctic around the world. Flight has given them the ability to survive in larger numbers and over a far wider range than they might without this gift. Some birds are capable of remaining on the wing for days at a time without rest except for the rest they find in soaring. The albatross glides for hours, using the air currents that flow over the ocean waves to support it and carry it, and so do some other birds of the sea. A vulture, drifting far overhead on a summer afternoon, seems at rest in the sky. But this is scarcely less remarkable than the short, erratic flight of the chickadee maneuvering through the branches of maple and oak trees in the nearby woods.

Migration Time

For bird watchers, the biggest and most rewarding show of the year comes during those seasons when birds, millions of them, are on the wing, traveling back and forth between wintering and nesting areas. In autumn, bird populations are at their annual peaks. Flights of warblers bring the treetops to life. Ducks drop in on nearby rivers, bays, and ponds, as new storms move them out of the north. Some birds make flights that seem incredible. The little ruby-throated hummingbird, weighing grams, may travel on whirring wings down across the continent to come eventually to the Gulf of Mexico. Then it follows a hazardous course across open water, a flight of five hundred miles without rest.

Meanwhile, the barn swallows that may have nested in Alaska are laboring along a nine-thousand-mile unmarked skyway toward their wintering area in South America. Along mountain ridges, coastlines, and river valleys move birds of prey, sharp-shinned hawks, redtails, vultures, and an occasional eagle. Shorebirds traveling in tight flocks, twisting and wheeling in unison like handfuls of chaff tossed in the wind, skim over bays and along shores on long-distance travels from far northern nesting grounds toward wintering areas in South America.

For species after species the grand journey is under way. Day and night the migrants continue to flow down the continent, sometimes making nonstop flights, but more often following a stop-and-go schedule that gives us the opportunity to see the birds as they pass through our neighborhoods.

Bristle-thighed curlew is a tireless traveler. This one was photographed in Hawaii, where it had just completed a 2,000-mile, nonstop trip from Alaska.

White ibis lives in salt marshes and mangrove forests along southern coasts.

Each migrant has its winter range and summer range, and each individual within the species may have its own territory, often returning, after an incredible trip across a route not marked in any way we can understand, to the very spot where it wintered or nested before. This is one of the mysteries of the bird's life, a puzzle that adds to the interest in following the life stories of these wild creatures.

These travels are essential to survival among the birds. The trip south in autumn carries the bird to where there will be food enough to see it through the winter. The magnificent whooping cranes that wing majestically down across the continent from wilderness nesting grounds in Canada to winter on the Texas Gulf Coast might withstand the cold of Canada, but there

In autumn, pintails and other ducks arrive by the millions in Tule Lake National Wildlife Refuge in the Klamath Basin of southern Oregon and northern California.

Canada goose, best known of all the wild geese, has been increasing in numbers and is often seen on ponds in and around cities.

they would starve to death long before spring brought a renewal of their northern foods. In Texas, they feast on a variety of foods, both animal and vegetable, and then in spring head north in good health and able to resume their nesting duties. Ducks that travel south leave behind in northern prairie ponds a world locked in ice.

But this does not mean that the birds are hungry when they leave or that hunger pangs tell them when to depart. Chances are excellent that they leave well fed and in good condition to make the arduous trip. Something besides

hunger triggers their departure, perhaps the shorter hours of daylight and resulting changes in the body's production of hormones.

Once on the wing the traveling birds must find their way. That cerulean warbler you suddenly glimpse, flitting through the maple trees, arrived in darkness following hours of unhesitating flight through the blackness, guided perhaps by the stars. How the migrating birds navigate, often traveling alone and over trails they have never flown before, has puzzled bird watchers since ancient times.

This navigation has been studied in a variety

of ways. When radar, developed during World War II, first began picking up blips made by the migrating birds, those watching the screens were thoroughly confused. Not knowing whether this was an enemy trick or a breakdown in the equipment, they searched for the answer. The clue was supplied by ornithologists. Thereafter, methods were developed to tell by radar the directions of flight and the density of migrating flocks, all of which added more clues to our understanding of the travels of the birds.

Meanwhile, other ornithologists were working out systems of counting nighttime migrants by pointing telescopes at the autumn moon and recording the number of birds seen crossing that yellow globe in the night. This is a fascinating plan that anyone with a spotting scope can practice. One can be as casual or scientific about it as one chooses, either content to simply watch the passing silhouettes against the harvest moon or to record the times, directions, and species involved in these observations.

In addition, bird watchers can search out the special migration events, the big shows that attract widespread attention and bring in viewers from distant points.

Examples include the annual return of the turkey vultures to their nesting ledges at Hinckley, Ohio, as regularly as clockwork, or the big show staged by Canada geese flocking into wildlife refuges by the thousands. Every family of bird watchers can keep its own record of the arrival and departure dates of birds that use the yard and garden each summer or winter, building through the years a family account of the remarkable schedules of the traveling birds.

Some species, however, do not migrate, and such birds as bobwhites and cardinals may spend their entire lives within half a mile of where they hatched. Some change their food habits with the seasons, feeding more heavily on insects in the summer and turning to seeds in winter.

There is at least one bird, the poor-will of the desert lands of the Southwest, that sometimes hibernates. It clings to a niche in a cliff, its life processes slow down, and there it passes the cold weeks until the world warms and the insects on which it lives are once again available to it.

How Fast Do Birds Fly?

One frequently argued subject is how fast various species of birds fly. Determining their speeds is not always easy. A bird may have one speed for cruising when not under extreme pressure, and a much faster speed to save its little feathered neck when a predator is pursuing it. The following speeds give the usual ranges for the flights of some well-known birds.

The rare peregrine falcon, fastest of all birds, builds its nest on wilderness cliffsides, but also on city skyscrapers where scientists have given young captive peregrines their freedom to rebuild their numbers.

Great blue heron	18-29 mph
Canada goose	20-60 mph
Mallard	26-60 mph
Turkey vulture	15-34 mph
Broad-winged hawk	20-40 mph
Bobwhite	28-49 mph
Ring-necked pheasant	27-38 mph
Killdeer	25-55 mph
Woodcock	5-13 mph
Mourning dove	26-41 mph
Barn swallow	20-46 mph
Crow	17-35 mph

The young fairy tern does not live in a nest. Its egg hatched on this bare branch where the chick must stay until old enough to fly.

In autumn, southbound flocks of geese, including these photographed at Horicon National Wildlife Refuge in Wisconsin, leave their northern nesting areas ahead of the ice.

Ecology

There is no bird sufficient unto itself, and the advanced bird watcher sees each bird as something more than four ounces of flesh, blood, and feathers. The kingfisher perched in a glass case inside the museum is not the same as the kingfisher hovering over the small stream about to dive on the flashing form of a fish. Alive, it is part of a living world where it has a niche into which it must fit and where it is related to all other elements of the world around it. The study of these relationships is the relatively young science of ecology, and it opens up new avenues to be explored because it lends understanding to the way birds live.

That kingfisher, the one fishing for its dinner, is more than a bird; it is a point on a circle of life that, like all circles, has no beginning and no ending. As much as anything the circle begins with sunlight. This is the source of energy tapped by the green plants. Through photosynthesis, plants convert this energy to forms they can use for growth. Then animals feed on these plants. The fish swimming in view of the kingfisher has grown because it fed either on plants or on smaller creatures that in turn drew nourishment from plants. The energy from the sun has moved through the plants into the animal world, and once there, from animal to animal until the kingfisher captures its prey. In its turn the kingfisher may fall prey to the hawk, or its young may be taken by a snake. All are parts of cycles of life in which kingfishers are only one part. Those parts of dead animals within this circle that are not consumed by other animals are attacked by the decomposers, and these tiny organisms bring about the decay that returns the materials to the earth, where they in turn help nourish other plants that again draw their energy from the sun. This briefly is the story of the kingfisher fitted to its world. Nothing can be taken from the cycle, or added to it, without having some effect on all other parts. Each species, whether house sparrow, bald eagle, or earthworm, plays an ecological role in relationship to the rest of the world around it. The

This great egret was photographed beside a Florida pond. These stately birds are widely distributed through the central part of the country during the breeding season.

Habitat destruction and over-hunting quickly reduced the passenger pigeon from millions to zero. This statue is part of a display that the Langdon Club, a naturalist organization, fostered at the Cincinnati Zoo in memory of the extinct pigeon.

kingfisher is part fish, part plant, part sunlight, and part air, with all these parts drawn from a giant natural bank account to which it also belongs. And that, as the ecologist will assure you, is a meaningful way to look at a bird.

This ecological approach means that each bird is fitted to a special habitat where it can find the water, food, and safety needed for its survival. The pileated woodpecker is tailored to life in the forest, and if you want to add the coot to your bird list, you will find it paddling about in shallow water, feasting on pondweed or duckweed. The study of ecology leaves no doubt that if the forest is cut down and the pond drained, not only do the trees and water vanish but the woodpeckers and the water birds that lived there must also disappear.

In addition to their widespread aesthetic appeal and their economic value, birds have been called indicators of the general health of the environment. Dr. Raymond F. Dasmann, a noted ecologist, teacher, and author, has said, "The wild birds and small animals of our city parks and gardens are going to become the most important wildlife in America." Wildlife to Dr. Dasmann, and other ecologists, becomes an index to the quality of urban living. "The city with the greatest variety and number of wild birds within it," he explains, "may well be the city with the highest-quality urban environment. A city with nothing but starlings and pigeons had better look to its planning and landscaping."

II

ACTIVITIES FOR BIRD WATCHERS

Scissor-tailed flycatcher is a popular common bird that nests in the south-central United States. *Karl H. Maslowski.*

Identifying Birds

Years ago the avid student of birds carried a gun. When he found a strange bird, he shot it, stuffed it into the pocket of his field coat, took it to his home, and studied it at his leisure. This was an acceptable procedure in frontier times. But fortunately times have changed, and bird watchers today would scarcely consider such an idea, even if it were legal, which, of course, it is not. Instead, the modern bird watcher is content to pursue his quarry, taking care to cause it no stress or injury, and identify it while getting only as close as his field skills and the natural wariness of the subject will permit. The challenge is all the greater.

This matter of identifying the birds may seem to the beginner, scanning his new bird guide, to be a staggering impossibility. We are told that perhaps 800 species of birds, residents or wanderers, are recorded for North America north of Mexico. With Mexico and Central America included, the list grows by another 1,000 species, grouped into nearly 100 families.

But the beginner can take some comfort from the fact that few people ever identify 700 species of birds in this country, and only rare and devoted individuals ever compile life lists of more than 600 of these species. Far more common, even among avid bird watchers, are life lists of 200 to 400 species.

Even the person who has never cracked a bird guide has a few species with which to begin a life list. Almost everyone knows the robin, pigeon (or rock dove), crow, bobwhite, house sparrow, and perhaps the starling, cardinal, blue jay, and a few more. Those who have learned these can soon learn to know other common birds, such species as the chickadee, titmouse, downy and hairy woodpeckers, Carolina wren, mourning dove, barn swallow, and scarlet tanager. Then the list can grow quickly through the

The white-throated sparrow is often seen around bird feeders in winter. Millet and other small grains are its favorite foods. *Karl H. Maslowski.*

Binoculars can be held steady by anchoring thumbs against cheeks.

first 100 or so species for the person who begins to look at birds seriously. Experienced bird watchers know some of the short cuts and fine points that have helped them become skilled in bird identification. It is best to start by going into the field with people who already know their birds well. Many communities have bird clubs, and the memberships often include the best naturalists in the area. These groups frequently conduct bird hikes where beginners are welcome.

Become proficient in the use of binoculars. Many a bird has winged its way out of sight while the person hoping to identify it fumbles with the binoculars trying to get them properly adjusted to both eyes or even fails to get them out of the case in time. Simply finding a bird through the binoculars can be a frustrating effort for the inexperienced. In one smooth movement binoculars come to the eyes, they are adjusted, and the subject is under study. Many prefer to shorten the strap on their binoculars until the glasses are carried only five or six inches beneath the chin. This not only keeps

them from banging against the body at belt level but also means a shorter distance to bring them into use. Binoculars should be protected from the rain. Otherwise they may have to be wiped dry before they can be used, and the time required may make the difference in whether or not the bird is identified. Most bird watchers do not carry binoculars in their cases while in the field. The case is too much trouble and too slow to use. Instead, binoculars can be protected from weather by carrying them under the coat, covering them with plastic, or equipping them with a leather flap made to cover the eyepieces.

Early efforts to identify a strange bird can be both fruitless and frustrating. There is a flash of movement in the green forest, a fumbling for binoculars, and a quick effort to turn the pages of the bird guide, searching hopefully for clues to the bird's identity. The smaller and quicker the bird, the bigger the problem. But there are tips that can increase your chances of making a

Tufted titmouse harvests its own dinner from a sunflower head hanging in a backyard tree.

Perhaps the best-known and least-loved bird in America is the house sparrow, an import from Europe. *Karl H. Maslowski.*

This immature tricolored heron was spotted in Florida's Corkscrew Swamp, a National Audubon Society sanctuary.

correct identification even on warblers, sparrows, and other small birds.

Rule one, according to John Oney, former director of the Cincinnati Nature Center, is not to take your eyes off the bird. "You may only see a flash of movement," says Oney. "Keep looking at it. Watch the bird as long as it is there." Notice its shape, the form of the bill, over-all colors, and special color markings. Then when it does fly, you will have memorized enough about it to help you find it in your field guide. Too often when people see a bird, they take their eyes off it to find their binoculars, then to seek clues in their bird guide. The binoculars should come to the eyes without losing sight of the bird. Study the bird until it flies or until you are satisfied, then consult the bird guide and check it against your observations.

Habitat can be a factor in identification. Some birds are normally found in open fields, others in the marshes. Shorebirds are found around water, woodpeckers near trees.

By studying bird books the beginner can soon learn to group birds by families, and this aids in identification. The birder who has a sound understanding of the family traits can often narrow down the possibilities rapidly when he sights a strange bird. Woodpeckers all cling to the sides of trees, using their tail feathers as a prop. Terns are known for their long slender wings and forked tails, while gulls generally have square or rounded tails. Swallows are rapid-flying birds that commonly feed on the wing over open fields.

Size is an important feature in identifying a bird. Widely known species are commonly used as comparisons. Birds are frequently described as similar in size to the house sparrow, robin, or crow.

Shapes are also significant in identification. The gallinaceous, or fowl-like, birds are heavy-bodied, have short bills, legs of medium length, and short wings. They are "chickenlike" in shape. By contrast, shorebirds are expected to be slender, longlegged birds with long pointed

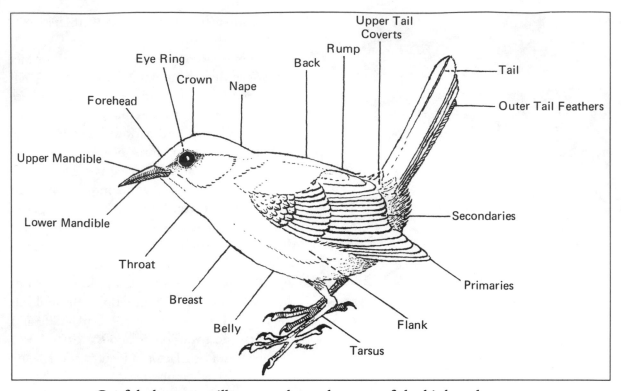

Careful observers will want to learn the parts of the bird so that special identification marks can be recorded in the field for later study. This drawing shows the accepted terms for describing various parts of a bird. Some birders carry such outline figures into the field and record notes or colors directly on the pictures. *Drawing by DeVere Burt.*

wings. The shapes of bills, feet, legs, and tails are particularly important features in identifying many kinds of birds, and consequently worth noting when studying a bird. Determine whether the bill is short, long, slender, thick, curved, or straight.

Color is sometimes, but not always, the key to identification. Some birds are distinctive in their coloring and quickly identified. The male Baltimore oriole, wearing black and brilliant orange marks, is quickly identified; the scarlet tanager, red with black wings, is easily recognized; the blue jay, the male goldfinch in summer plumage, and the indigo bunting are also quickly known by their color markings. But frequently birds are not seen in good light, or their colors may seem to vary in different light condi-

tions. Against the sky the colors may be difficult to determine. The observer needs to learn differences in plumage between males and females, immature and adult, or seasonal differences. Male goldfinches that fly around the garden and weedy fields, wearing brilliant yellows and blacks in summer, can go unrecognized in their drab grayish yellows at the winter feeder. Field observers often make notes on colors and patterns of birds they observe. This is made easier by learning the exterior parts of a bird and using this knowledge as a guide in noting color patterns. A notation that a bird had "white upperwing coverts" or "white outer tail feathers" might provide the information needed to nail down an identification. Aside from colors, bird field guides frequently point out other key iden-

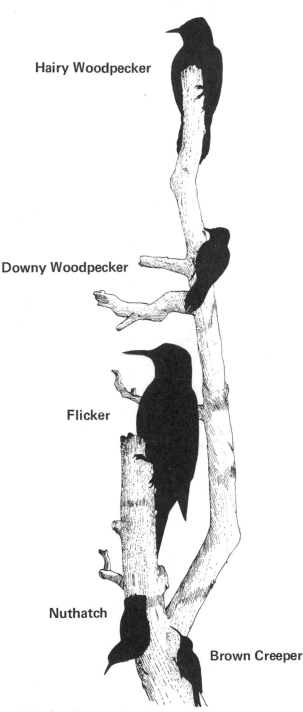

Hairy Woodpecker

Downy Woodpecker

Flicker

Nuthatch

Brown Creeper

Woodpeckers and other species of tree-climbing birds can be separated by comparing sizes, shapes, and habits. These drawings will aid in identifying the more common of these woodland birds. *Drawing by DeVere Burt.*

tification marks. Among the features that birders watch for are wingbars, eye rings, crests, tail length, and size and shape of the bill. Studying bird pictures helps the observer learn to recognize features that set whole families of birds apart from each other.

The bird watcher should also be a bird listener who understands that except for their songs many birds would be missed completely. At times, birds can be heard when no amount of slipping through the underbrush will bring the elusive little creatures into range of the binoculars. I recall a misty, wet morning in a forest of giant ferns on the island of Hawaii when ornithologist Winston E. Banko, an endangered-species specialist with the U.S. Fish and Wildlife Service, was attempting to introduce me to some of the forest birds native to the island. We followed a twisting trail over fallen stumps until I was completely lost. Every few minutes Banko would stop to listen. I studied the treetops, jungles of fragile green leaves silhouetted against the gray sky.

From somewhere above us a flutelike note filtered through the leaves. Then a different song greeted us. I was told that we had heard the apapane, iiwi, and elepaio. I hadn't seen the birds. Neither had Banko. But because he had identified their songs, he was able to record them. There are days, he explained, when he sees perhaps no more than 5 percent of the birds he records in those forests.

In a forest in Ohio, Missouri, or New York, the bird watcher may hear, but not see, red-eyed vireos, nuthatches, pileated woodpeckers, towhees, and others. Then, in the nearby open fields, he may catch the high-pitched notes of the grasshopper sparrow without seeing the bird.

Some birds tell their names. Bobwhite. Killdeer. Pewee. Whip-poor-will. Others tell you nothing. Some people have tried, perhaps with moderate success, to write the songs of birds in musical scales. A more common method, and one more useful to most birders, is

California gull photographed at rest on a pond in Yellowstone National Park.

an attempt to translate the notes of the song into words that are easily remembered. If the cardinal sounds to you like a man whistling for his dog, or the Carolina wren seems to say "*tea-kettle, tea-kettle, tea-kettle,*" and the barred owl calls, "*who cooks for you, who cooks for you all,*" you are likely to remember and recognize these songs better than you might without such associations of words. Songs and calls can be learned from bird recordings available today. In addition to providing pleasant entertainment in their own right, these recordings are well worth their cost as teaching devices.

In addition, knowing the birds' habits and habitat will aid in identification: whether they are normally found in trees, what part of the forest canopy they occupy, where they nest,

whether their flight pattern is straight or undulating, whether they flap their wings constantly or flap and glide, and whether they are usually seen in flocks or singly.

A good part of identification is understanding the probabilities of seeing a bird where and when you think you might have spotted it. Some birds, such as the downy and hairy woodpeckers, are permanent year-round residents through much of the country. Others nest in one region and spend their winters in another. In addition, rare visitors are frequently reported by bird watchers in areas where they are seldom expected. Some may arrive as accidentals on the heels of a storm, while some, including the snowy owl, may be forced south in unusual winters by food short-

Yellow-billed cuckoo is a tireless harvester of insects, such as the annual cicada which this one feeds to its young ones. *Karl H. Maslowski.*

ages. Bird guides give information on ranges of each species. Observations that do not fit these standard patterns are usually suspect unless corroborated by skilled naturalists. Some birds are extremely rare, even within their normal range, automatically reducing the probabilities of sighting them.

Bird identification and the proficiency one acquires in knowing birds has no boundaries, no fixed ending. It is one of those rare activities in today's world that can be adjusted to any pace the birder wants to follow, with the knowledge that there are always new challenges and exciting new birding possibilities in any part of the country or around the world. There are few pressures built into bird study. It is one of those welcome areas in which you can do as much or as little as you care to.

Bird Guides

No one remembers all the details about all the wild birds out there. A pocket-sized reference book, a bird guide that reveals with words and pictures the fine points separating similar birds, becomes almost as essential as binoculars. Even highly skilled birders keep a bird guide handy. These are more than field guides; they are good for home study anytime.

When I first became interested in birds, there was no comprehensive bird guidebook on the market. The earliest ones I recall were written by Chester A. Reed. These were published in 1928 by Doubleday. One was called *Land Birds East of the Rockies,* but there were others in the series and all were available in what we then called the "ten cent store" or the "five and dime." I no longer recall the price, but I do remember that the same Woolworth store sold a large ice cream cone for five cents.

With a page size of three by five inches, these little books were small enough to fit into a boy's pants pocket. Each page was devoted to a single bird, with half of the page going to a color drawing and the other half to a mini-essay in very small type about the bird, its habitat, and habits.

These little pioneering bird books are interesting today as antiques but also because they contrast so sharply with modern bird guides, which are packed with color pictures, range maps, song renditions, and detailed pointers on identification. Furthermore, today's bird guides include not just sixty or so of the more common birds but essentially all the birds known for the areas covered, arranged by families so the bird in question is easily found. These modern bird guides have much in common. They show North American birds in full color. They tell where they are normally seen in various seasons, often the habitat types they frequent, and the identifying marks that enable an observer to separate birds that might, at first glance, look alike. Although considerably larger than my earliest Chester A. Reed book, today's guides still fit into a coat pocket.

Today there are at least three highly popular bird guide books. Perhaps the one I refer to most often is *Birds of North America - A Guide to Field Identification,* by Chandler S. Robbins, Bertel Bruun, and Herbert S. Zim. It is illustrated by famed bird artist Arthur Singer and published by Golden Press.

In addition, I often use *Field Guide to the Birds of North America,* published by the National Geographic Society. This book is slightly bulkier than most common bird guide books but it is an excellent choice whether carried in the field or used at home.

Perhaps the best known field guides to the birds are those by Roger Tory Peterson. His 1934 book, *A Field Guide to the Birds,* dealt with the birds of eastern North America and was the first field guide of the modern genre. Peterson later produced a companion volume on the birds of the West, and these bird books became the foundation of a whole series of excellent

"Peterson" guides on wild plants and animals.

There is also the *Audubon Land Bird Guide* and a companion volume *Audubon Water Bird Guide,* by Richard H. Pough. These books offer a more detailed text than do some guides.

One set of bird guides uses color photographs instead of paintings to help identify birds. These are *The Audubon Society Field Guide to North American Birds,* with separate books for the eastern and western regions. The text in these books is excellent, but many birders find that paintings serve better than photographs as field guide illustrations.

In addition, there are numerous state and regional bird guides. New bird books appear every year. There are enough regional bird guides to fill thirty pages of the catalog published by American Birding Association, P.O. Box 6599, Colorado Springs, CO 80934. The ABA catalog groups these books according to nation, state, province, or region. Available also are videos and tapes that can help birders learn to recognize birds by sight or sound.

Traveling birders headed for distant lands can find bird guide books for numerous foreign countries. These are carried in good nature shops, including those operated by nature centers or museums of natural history. Or they can be ordered from catalogs or through a bookstore.

Keeping a bird guide dry on field trips can be a problem. Some birders make a belt pouch to fit the book, and these are sometimes available commercially. A plastic bag will solve the moisture problem.

Understanding Scientific Names

One of my favorite birds of the forests and thickets is the ruffed grouse. But it may not be recognized by that name at all in parts of its range. In Michigan, it is called partridge or "pat," and in the forested mountains of North Carolina, it is known to some as the pheasant.

Meanwhile, another favorite, the pileated woodpecker, may be called by different names depending on where it happens to be seen. Some mountain people have long known it as the woodcock or even the "Lord God woodpecker." There are other and more confusing

Widely distributed cliff swallow *Hirundo pyrrhonota* builds mud nests in colonies beneath bridges and the eaves of buildings.

samples of the same species carrying a variety of common names. This explains why birds have not only common names but also scientific names written in Latin form. Whether you are a scientist or not, you may occasionally want to check birds by their scientific names. It is not difficult. Bird guides commonly carry scientific as well as common names.

A great Swedish naturalist, Carolus Linnaeus (1707-78), worked out this worldwide system by which a species is commonly given two scientific names. It has a genus name followed by the species name. They are always written in italics. The first letter of the genus name is capitalized, and the species name is written in lower case. A third name indicates a subspecies. The same system of scientific nomenclature is used for all species of plants and animals.

The American Ornithologists' Union *Checklist of North American Birds* is generally considered the last word on the correct names of American birds. Birds' names are not static. New editions of the AOU check list include changes in both common and scientific names.

The advantage of a system of scientific names is obvious. Pileated woodpecker becomes *Dryocopus pileatus* around the world. The chickenlike bird of the eastern woodlands may be ruffed grouse, pheasant, or partridge, but everywhere it is *Bonasa umbellus*. Ornithologists in any part of the world would know if you said *"Passer domesticus"* that you referred to the house sparrow.

Seeing More Birds

Some people see more birds than others do. To a surprisingly large degree such success in finding birds can grow out of a person's ability to move about unobtrusively outdoors, fitting into the wild scene and not startling the wildlife with every movement.

Skilled hunters who are also bird watchers know that bird stalking is good practice for game stalking. In the fields and along the streams wild birds want no part of us, and approaching them closely enough for a good view tests the bird watcher's outdoor skill.

Choose clothing that blends into the surroundings. Birds see color. Bright reds, yellows, and oranges show up through the woods alerting birds to the fact that something strange has come into their territory. This makes them uneasy and nervous. Somber browns and greens are better choices. Clothing can also be noisy. Plastic or rubberized garments make more unnatural noises rubbing against brush than do natural fibers. Wool is especially quiet. Loose clothing that flaps in the wind can alert birds.

Chances are that birds you come close to will know of your presence regardless of how you dress and how quietly you move. The eye of the bird is a marvelous creation. But the better you fit into the surroundings, the more chance you have of keeping the birds calm long enough to work your way up close to them. Quick movements mean danger to wildlife. Rapid walking, sudden turning of the head, quick pointing, lifting the binoculars rapidly, can all serve to alert

and frighten birds. Staying in one place for five minutes, perhaps resting against a tree or sitting on a log, may bring out birds you would otherwise miss. This is a matter of attitude. The birder

This popular viewing tower, known as "the owl's roost," was erected on the Okefenokee National Wildlife Refuge in Georgia, especially for birders.

who remembers that he or she is a foreigner in the woods and fields, as far as the birds are concerned, will find it easier to approach the wildlife living there. Learn how to move unobtrusively in the outdoors, fit into the natural picture, and almost certainly you will be rewarded with a longer list of birds and more interesting natural observations over the years than the person content to crash through the underbrush.

These are skills to help you get closer to birds. There are also techniques that bird watchers use to make the birds come to them. Years ago someone learned that a kissing sound made by sucking the back of the hand will often, but not always, draw small birds into view, perhaps from curiosity.

During World War II, an American soldier serving in Italy became interested in the bird calls used by Italian hunters, who shoot small songbirds for food. From one of these Italian bird calls the American adapted a squeaking call to test back in the United States. It worked.

Warblers, vireos, and other small birds came in readily. Today it is known as the Audubon Bird Call, and it can be purchased from birding supply stores or the National Audubon Society, 700 Broadway, New York, NY 10003.

American Indians learned long ago that wild turkeys respond to artificial calls made from bone, slate, or wood. Several versions are available in sporting-goods stores, and although they are usually sold to turkey hunters, there is no rule that says they cannot be equally satisfying to the nonhunter who wants to add the wild turkey to his or her life list or bring the strutting gobbler close for pictures. The experience of calling up a gobbler during the warming weeks of spring can be exhilarating. Other calls are made for doves and waterfowl, and bird watchers can use them without worrying about closed seasons.

Some bird watchers have found that a plastic owl, obtainable from sporting-goods stores, will draw small birds out of hiding and bring them swarming down to attack the "predator."

Photographing Birds

Modern sophisticated cameras have brought nature photography into a new age. Pioneering outdoor photographers shouldered huge box-type cameras and covered their head and shoulders with black cloth when making a picture. Today anyone can be outfitted with a miniature hand-held camera that fits into a coat pocket. This does not, however, automatically mean that modern pictures are always superior to those turned out by the early photographers. I often think of the pictures made by Dr. Alfred M. Bailey, who became Director of the Denver Museum of Natural History.

In 1912 Bailey traveled with a working team of biologists to the remote little unoccupied leeward islands of Hawaii. There he made black-and-white bird pictures using a simple folding camera borrowed from a friend and not even tested before leaving home. But his albatross pictures still rank high for their photographic quality as well as for what they tell us about the birds of the islands. Bailey, and many others, have proved that good bird photography is partly in the equipment, but largely in the eye of the photographer.

The standard equipment today is a 35mm single-lens reflex camera and a variety of lenses. The well-equipped photographer may outfit his camera with motor drive and autofocus 400mm or 600mm lenses with extension tubes that bring small birds in to where the image is large enough to fill the frame with a robin at fifteen feet. Such equipment enables the photographer to reach out from a distance great enough to avoid spooking the subject. This is important because it increases the chances of making satisfactory pictures, but also because it helps avoid harassing wildlife and disturbing its daily routine.

Almost universally, bird photographers today work with color film. For most of us it is a good idea to find films that give good results and stick with them, keeping in mind that high-speed films may be needed for poor light conditions.

Film, especially color film, should be fresh when used. It is stamped with an expiration date, beyond which its quality is questionable. There may be leeway in the dating, but I take

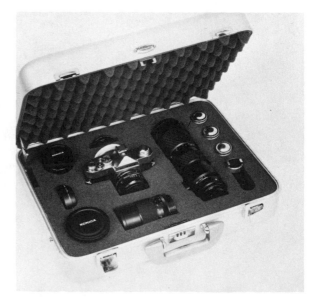

Strong aluminum case lined with soft foam protects delicate camera equipment in the field.

no chances on this. I don't want to shoot a rare bird or unusual event only to find the film quality lower than it should have been.

Storage of film is important. Film should be stored where it will be cool and dry. Color film allowed to become too hot from direct sunlight, riding in a glove compartment, or lying on a heater or radiator may have the colors ruined. Many professional photographers keep their unopened film in the freezer until a few hours before using it or packing it for a trip. This does not mean that film has to be rushed out to the field, exposed, then hurried back to the laboratory or it will be a total loss. It is not that critical. I have often carried film in the deserts without suffering noticeable loss of quality from heat. But I worried about the film, kept it in the shade, and did not delay processing any longer than was essential. Exposed color film will deteriorate more quickly than unexposed film.

Laysan albatross, nesting in the Hawaiian Islands, watches over her single fuzzy chick. These tireless fliers spend much of the year at sea, coming ashore only to raise their young.

This colony of white pelicans nests on a wildlife refuge island in Montana and migrates south, to better fishing grounds, for the winter.

Exposure is a puzzler for many a photographer. The latitude is not great, and transparencies either too light (overexposed) or too dark (underexposed) can make disappointing slide presentations as well as pictures that editors will not want to buy, if you are aiming at publication of your bird pictures. If there is a choice, the slightly underexposed color transparency is generally more acceptable than one that is overexposed.

With some modern cameras this exposure problem is partly solved by built-in self-activating exposure meters that automatically set the camera for the film speed. But other cameras must be set for exposure by adjusting the shut-ter speed and the opening in the behind the lens diaphragm which controls the amount of light passing through to the film.

There are several ways of determining the correct exposure. Each roll of film comes with directions, and the shutter speeds and *f*-stops listed on these instruction sheets are generally good guides. But an exposure meter also becomes an important part of the wildlife photographer's outfit, particularly because he will frequently be working under adverse light conditions in shaded places.

After you have set the combination of *f*-stop and shutter speed, assuming that your equip-

National wildlife refuges administered by the U.S. Fish and Wildlife Service are excellent locations for finding birds and photographing them.

Brown booby nesting in the Hawaiian Islands shades her single naked chick from the hot sun.

ment is not fully automatic, there remains only one additional adjustment to make in the usual circumstance, and this is to be certain the camera is focused. Check the depth of field to be certain all elements of the picture you want sharp will be sharp. Generally the faster the shutter speed at which you can shoot the better, if the resulting depth of focus is adequate.

This brings us, however, to the basic question of when not to shoot a picture. My rule here is to shoot more than I think I should. If the subject is a rarity, shoot it even if the light is wretched. At the worst you will have to discard the shot, and at the best you could come up with an unforgettable picture dramatically lighted. Too frequently, photographers fail to extend themselves and push their equipment beyond the predictable limits. Some of the best pictures are made early and late in the day and at other times when the light conditions may not be optimum.

Long lenses are difficult to hold steady. Cam-

When no tripod is available, the bird photographer should make use of rocks or other secure objects to steady his telephoto lens.

era movement will blur the picture, and the more the lens magnifies the scene, the greater movement is likely to be magnified. Often the photographer can find a rock, post, or tree against which to brace his camera. Then, while holding his breath, he carefully depresses the shutter release, taking care not to jolt the camera at that instant. Where a tripod can be used, use it, and the more rigid the tripod the better. The tripod is quality insurance.

Sometimes a certain amount of subject movement adds to the picture. The blurred wings of the hummingbird gets across the idea of speed, providing the rest of the bird is frozen in motion at the instant of exposure. To stop a bird in flight calls for high speeds, perhaps a 500th of a second minimum for slow-flying birds, 1,000th or faster for speeding birds. Sometimes good pictures of flying birds are obtained by moving the camera to follow the bird at its own speed and shooting while the camera is in motion. Done properly, and with a bit of luck, this can produce a picture in which everything but the bird is blurred, making it obvious that the bird is traveling.

If you are buying new camera equipment for an important trip, remember to run several rolls of film through it and develop them before departing. One bird photographer friend of mine prepared for his first trip beyond the Arctic Circle by purchasing a new camera. It was still carrying its first roll of color film when it reached the tundra. The results were less than the traveler had hoped for, and he vowed that never again would he fail to test his equipment before making such a trip.

Outdoor photographers sometimes put their equipment to hard use in hazardous situations, and for this reason must give thought to protec-

The late Frederick Kent Truslow, shown here at work in Everglades National Park for *National Geographic Magazine,* **gained fame as a bird photographer after giving up a successful business career to pursue his main interest.**

tion of cameras and lenses. Personally I never purchase, or at least soon discard, the leather camera cases provided by the manufacturers. They get in the way. While a photographer is opening his camera case, the bird he hopes to photograph is blue-skying it off to the next farm. Instead, I carry my photographic outfit in a sizable aluminum case equipped with foam pads which can be cut with individual spaces to accommodate the various items or a soft canvas case with padded compartments. Such cases should keep out most dust and moisture and are shock-resistant by virtue of the padding built into them. I am not fond of the square leather or plastic shoulder bags. There is no really comfortable and easy way to carry a complete camera system including all the lenses. For climbing under difficult situations or for long hikes, I fit my aluminum case into a Duluth-style backpack or repack the equipment into a day pack.

There are occasions when the photographer can approach his wild subjects closely and photograph them at his leisure. But these are rare days. I recall a photographic session on an island in the Pacific where sea birds, unexposed to mammalian predators and seemingly unafraid of man, nested in profusion and all the photographer had to do was sit in the sun a few feet from the nesting birds and make as many pictures as he cared to shoot. The birds did not fly or run away and seemed to dare anyone to come within pecking range of their long spike bills. This is the kind of situation that photographers dream about, and if all nature photography were so simple, a single lens might suffice.

More common is the situation in which you want to capture the image of a gull on the wing, a soaring hawk, or a pileated woodpecker landing on its distant nest tree. Or you want to move in on your subject until you are inches from it, photographing perhaps the nest or eggs of a hummingbird or a small woodland wild flower. All such situations demand more than the usual standard lens will deliver.

The answer is to start with basic equipment to which you can add new items as the need arises and money is available. This means beginning with a camera capable of taking interchangeable lenses. The first lens to buy, and the one with which the camera is most likely equipped when new, is the standard lens. In a 35mm camera this will be a 50 or 55mm lens.

The bird photographer needs telephoto lenses, which reach out and enable him to photograph subjects he cannot otherwise approach. For 35mm photography I find two of these longer lenses adequate for covering most situations. The longest is a 400mm lens. This is a widely used telephoto lens among 35mm camera owners. It is best used from a tripod.

In addition, the nature photographer frequently uses a medium-length telephoto lens. One answer is the zoom lens built to offer a variety of focal lengths within its designated range. A commonly used zoom, for 35mm cameras, ranges from 90mm to 210mm. There are other choices, however, including 55mm to 135mm, and 85mm to 205mm. These are highly versatile lenses. Ordinarily they permit the photographer to focus his camera, then compose a picture by moving a lens ring to increase or decrease the size of the image and control the amount of background.

So far the 35mm outfit includes three lenses. One more that is highly useful is a wide-angle lens. A moderately wide-angle lens, such as 35mm, is sometimes used as a standard lens. The wide-angle lens may be valuable for shooting landscapes. It also gives a greater depth of field, and focusing becomes less critical. But it can also be important to the nature photographer for close-up work. Another place where wide-angle lenses are valuable, of course, is in making pictures inside enclosures or buildings, or for making the inevitable reunion snapshots and getting all the relatives on both ends of the line into the picture.

With these lenses, standard, zoom, long telephoto, and wide angle, the average outdoor photographer can handle almost any photo situation encountered. For the photographer building his list of equipment a piece at a time, I would suggest starting with camera and either 35mm, 50mm, or 55mm lens. Next add either the zoom or long telephoto, finally a wider-angle lens. For those not satisfied with this range of lenses there are many additional ones available. One thing to avoid, however, is the temptation to overequip yourself with a long list of items that may seldom be used. Some photographers gather more pleasure from owning equipment in wide variety than from the photos they create. Though there is nothing wrong with this, especially from the camera salesman's point of view, neither is there a need for several cases of equipment for the average camera-carrying bird watcher.

There are ways to cut down the investment in building a set of camera equipment. Even professionals do not always insist that their lenses carry the same name as their camera. There are lines of reasonably priced lenses made to fit many popular 35mm cameras.

Some cameras come complete with built-in exposure meters, which can be excellent, especially if they are of the spot meter design. Auxiliary exposure meters are important for measuring light under difficult conditions, such as the dull light of the forest or the shaded area where a bird has built its nest.

Some cameras can be equipped with motors that advance the film and enable the photographer to make several exposures per second. Motor drives are available for relatively expensive cameras. Sport photographers frequently use them, but they can also be valuable to the nature photographer. By pressing a button the photographer makes a whole series of pictures of two male cardinals engaged in a territorial combat or a heron fishing for its breakfast.

Nature photographers frequently need supplemental light if they are to make sharp pictures. Flash equipment comes in a wide variety. Some of the latest flash outfits are cigarette-pack size and do remarkable work. For more light you may need more powerful equipment. Some units automatically adjust light volume to match the film and the camera setting. A visit to the camera shop will give an overview of the flash equipment available.

In nature photography a knowledge of the subject matter can be at least as important as a knowledge of cameras. You may know all there is to learn about your equipment, and this is good, but if you know the ways of the animal you are photographing, you are more likely to create a set of outstanding pictures of it and its way of life.

When photographing action, remember that many kinds of action have an instant when they peak out. Photographing a sandhill crane in its courtship dance provides a moment when the leaping bird reaches its maximum height, and at that point, before it begins to settle back to earth, there comes an instant when the bird is almost motionless. It becomes predictable to the seasoned photographer, and similar peaks of movement can be found in many actions where film speeds or light conditions make subject movement troublesome.

Bird photographers frequently try to fill the frame with a bird. But if the object is to show the bird or nest in its natural surroundings, the photographer has the opportunity to work for pleasing composition. The composition is usually better if the main subject is not in the dead center of the frame. Other material included in the picture should, where possible, be relevant. Otherwise the secondary objects distract from the main object.

If you plan to show your slides to an audience, even a family audience, remember that, as one of my lecture circuit friends says, "The show starts when the pictures are made."

Bird Rescue

Most birds that come under the immediate care of people are either injured so badly they cannot fly or are so young they are helpless. The young bird you are worried about may not need help. Most of the time it does not. During the nesting season, the young are often found out of the nest. If they are about to fly, this may be quite natural, and they may still be under the care of their parents. If so, it is definitely a mistake to take them into custody. The best general rule is to tell yourself that birds have been getting along on their own for longer than there have been people around to "help" them, and they should be left to their own devices. From a harsh biological point of view the loss of one more young bird of any moderately common species is insignificant in the over-all survival of the species. Wild creatures, including birds, normally overproduce. Most young normally perish before their first birthday. This is a natural insurance policy allowing the species to get through all the hard times it faces.

But if the little bird is so young it definitely needs help, place it back in the nest as quickly and gently as possible. Then it is best for the good Samaritan to depart, so the parent birds can return and take up the bird-raising chores in which they are expert.

To take the young bird under your care with the intention of raising it is to commit yourself to a long and tedious assignment. If you are successful, you will have fed it every few hours for many days or weeks. There is also the legal point; federal and state laws make it illegal to hold nearly any wild bird in captivity unless you have a special permit, and non-scientists can rarely get such permits. Check with your local conservation officer.

Knowing all this, let us discuss briefly the foods suitable for a young bird. The one most commonly recommended is boiled egg yolk. Baby cereal is sometimes fed. So is hamburger, ground very fine, or even bread and milk. Pet shops sometimes sell live foods for birds. Hawks and owls normally need whole small animals, complete with hair and bones. Captive birds should be given a drop or two of vitamin supplement or cod-liver oil at least once a week.

Cleanliness is important in the living conditions for young birds just as for any other animal. Supply the captive with fresh water in some manner that will prevent it from being soaked or injured. Pet stores also have equipment to meet this need.

The mature bird that needs help is easily identified. If it cannot fly well, there is something wrong. One common problem in the bird world these days is oil on the feathers. This is a threat to birds living around water, especially bays and harbors where there are oil installations or where offshore winds may move in petroleum products from any of the numerous spills, large and small, that occur each year. Major oil spills often kill large numbers of birds.

Birds not killed outright by the oil can sometimes be saved. During the famous Santa Barbara spill in 1969, dozens of concerned citizens labored to collect the oiled birds and attempt to clean them so they could be released back into the wild.

This happened on a grand scale following that March night in 1989 when the Exxon Valdez crumpled her steel hull on the jagged rocks of a reef in Prince William Sound. By the time I arrived, hours later with other journalists from around the world, the volunteer animal rescue workers were organized and making their way toward Alaska.

Boats were soon bringing in birds with so much oil on them that they were scarcely recognizable. Washing stations were set up, equipment flown in, procedures standardized. Some of the oiled birds survived, but far more perished. How much good this did for the birds remains open to speculation, but it left the bird washers feeling better. They had done their best to rescue wild creatures caught up in a human-caused tragedy.

Oil-soaked birds tend to swim toward the beach because, once contaminated, they begin to sink. Besides, the oiled bird is probably too heavy to fly. If the oil spill is an extensive one, and the number of birds contaminated is large, the rescue will call for co-ordinated and organized efforts of many volunteers and professionals. Anyone attempting to capture such a bird, even for humane purposes, should understand that federal laws and treaties governing migratory wildlife and state laws covering resident species make the holding of such birds an illegal act. But in an emergency authorities frequently work with bird rescue crews to save as many of the threatened birds as possible.

Long-handled nets will help in the capture of oiled birds. Some birds are so heavy with oil during a spill that they can be easily picked up by hand. Slightly contaminated birds should not be run down with boats or pursued to a state of exhaustion. Left alone, they may recover. Captured birds should be placed in holding boxes that can be kept dark, ventilated, and neither too cool nor too hot. If there are official bird rescue stations set up within reasonable traveling distance, get the captured birds to this location as quickly as possible.

Throughout these steps, the bird should be handled firmly but gently. Covering the eyes may help calm the bird, and this can be important because excessive stress may be as hazardous as oil.

To release the washed birds into the wild would condemn them to an early death. Weeks may pass before their natural oils restore their feather condition, and during that time they must be kept out of the water and provided with food and drinking water in shallow pans and housed at temperatures of 55° to 65°.

Throughout these procedures the guidance of an ornithologist or veterinarian or local conservation officer can improve the chances for the birds to survive. Again, such projects must normally be authorized by wildlife authorities. These trained workers will also be the best judges on suitable places to release birds that survive the ordeal of being rescued, cleaned, and rehabilitated.

Picture windows claim large numbers of birds each year. Birds as large as barred owls and as small as warblers strike windows. Prevention of these collisions is covered elsewhere in this book, but assuming such a crash occurs, there is always the question of what to do with the injured bird. Often the birds need to be left alone. They should, however, be placed where they will be unavailable to neighborhood cats while helpless. An outside area is best if there is, for example, a deck or windowsill where the bird can be placed out of the sun and wind as well as danger from predators. If only stunned, it may begin to revive in a few minutes and soon fly away without the added stress that handling by humans or enclosure in a box might add to its troubles.

If it was a high-speed collision, the bird's chances may be slender. Broken necks and internal injuries are common from these head-on collisions. Seldom does such a bird suffer only a broken wing or leg.

Broken wings or legs usually mean death to a bird in the wild, and to help it avoid this early end people have frequently attempted to set the broken bone until it can heal.

In general, adult birds with no obvious external injuries, but incapable of flight after thirty minutes or so of recovery time, will probably die whatever the treatment offered.

Bird Banding

Bird watchers, ancient as well as modern, have observed with a sense of wonder the travels of birds with the changing seasons. And it was not until men learned how to mark individual birds so they could be later identified that we began solving many of the riddles. Today great stores of knowledge have been accumulated as a result of the banding of birds, or as it is called in England, ringing. You may someday find one of these special birds, and if you do, you will recognize it by the lightweight aluminum band it wears on one leg. If the bird is dead, the band should be removed, straightened out, taped to a piece of heavy paper, then sent to the Bird Banding Laboratory, U.S. Fish and Wildlife Service, Laurel, Md. 20708, along with the following information:

1. Your name and address (plainly printed).
2. All numbers and letters on the band.
3. The date you found the band.
4. The place you found the band (mileage and directions from the nearest town, with county and state).
5. How you found the band (on a bird found dead, shot, or taken in some other way).

No such band should ever be removed from a live bird. The person who for any reason has such a banded live bird in hand should instead copy the number, then release the captive. The information should then be sent to the Migratory Bird Research Laboratory. Some of the smallest bands have the numbers on the inside because there is not enough room on the outside. These likewise should never be removed from a living bird just to discover what the number might be. Instead, let the bird go on its way.

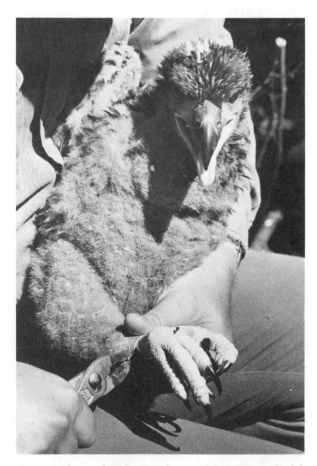

By marking birds, such as this young bald eagle, with aluminum bands, scientists have mapped migration routes.

When these reports reach Laurel, Maryland, they are processed by a bank of computers and a small crew of professional government workers who do nothing but work with bird-banding information. In this laboratory are kept all banding data from the United States and Canada. These millions of records reveal the flyways of waterfowl, the travels of the bald eagle, and the wanderings of a host of other birds of almost every species known to the continent. There are remarkable stories of the lives and travels of wild birds hidden in these extensive files. One red-winged blackbird shot in North

This newly banded indigo bunting now becomes part of the records preserved by the Fish and Wildlife Service Bird Banding Laboratory in Maryland.

In 1803, John James Audubon tied silver threads around the legs of a brood of phoebes (above), and this is believed to be the first time North American birds were banded. At least two of Audubon's marked birds returned the following spring.

Carolina was known to have lived fourteen years from the day it was banded in New York. A banded black duck lived seventeen years before it was finally shot. A barn swallow banded in Indiana was found in Brazil. Meanwhile, the unraveling story of the Arctic tern revealed that this tireless traveler normally makes an annual round trip of 22,000 miles traveling between its nesting area near the Arctic Circle and its wintering grounds in Antarctica, the longest known bird migration of all.

Bird banding in this country was once an unorganized hobby. Anyone who banded birds did so according to his own plan. Eventually, in 1909, bird banders organized into the American Bird Banding Association. The work of the group, however, practically stopped during World War I. Following that conflict government biologists took over supervising of bird banding in North America, and it has been an official function of the United States and Canada since

1920. Today there are about two thousand official bird banders in North America. The Bird Banding Laboratory supplies them annually with a million or more aluminum bands in nearly two dozen sizes. There are bands small enough to fit hummingbirds and large enough to fit trumpeter swans. About half of the official banders are state and federal government biologists.

Bird banders capture young birds still in the nest or adult birds either in traps or in very thin, almost invisible, nets known as mist nets. Either one, properly handled, will not injure the birds. Possession of mist nets is illegal without a special permit.

If you would like to be a bird bander, you must be at least eighteen years old and be skilled in identification of all common birds in their various seasonal plumages, as well as explain how the banding will contribute to a research project. Then you must have the endorsement of at least three well-known ornithologists or outstanding naturalists.

The Christmas Bird Count

As Christmas Day 1900 approached, Frank M. Chapman explained to a number of his bird-watching friends a special plan that had been taking shape in his mind. Chapman, a New Jersey-born self-trained ornithologist who became chairman of the famed Bird Department of the American Museum of Natural History in New York City, and who was one of the founders of the National Audubon Society, had decided to spend all of Christmas Day hiking the fields and counting birds. Twenty-six other bird watchers agreed to spend the day in the fields. They covered twenty-five small areas of the country stretching from the Atlantic to the Pacific. This was the beginning of what was to become a major annual event in the world of birding.

Today the annual Christmas bird count, with nearly a century of history behind it, is growing. In one recent year an army of 35,450 bird watchers, men, women and youngsters, hiked the fields, woods, and waterways in more than 1,500 areas. They searched for birds in all fifty states as well as Canada, Central and South America, the Caribbean, and the Pacific Islands. They counted in North America alone some 54 million birds of 587 species. In addition, 7,236 people counted the birds coming to their feeders. The census takers recording the greatest numbers of species were in the tropical rain forest areas—some with lists totaling more than 300 kinds of birds. Meanwhile, in the Far North, others had searched throughout the day

with only a few ptarmigan, snowy owls, and ravens to report.

This annual search for the birds of the Western Hemisphere brings built-in hardships. In many parts of the country the December weather is bitterly cold. Birders, according to the rules, must stay in the field for at least eight hours. Some start out shortly after midnight on the appointed day, hoping to record owls and other nocturnal birds. They travel by whatever means are best fitted to the area they must cover. Some reach their census areas on snow-mobiles, helicopters, bicycles, golf carts, automobiles and trucks, boats of all kinds, and most of all on human feet.

All these bird watchers must follow the same set of rules established by the National Audubon Society, which is responsible for conducting the annual census out of its offices in New York City with the cooperation of the U.S. Fish and Wildlife Service. A group of bird watchers may have as many individuals as it cares to. They work under a leader. They need not conduct their census on Christmas Day but each year the official framework is from about ten days before to ten days after Christmas. Each of these groups searches for birds in a fifteen-mile-diameter area. The group leader determines how the bird watchers will be divided and where they will spend each part of the day to see the maximum number of species and individuals.

By evening of the census day these fieldwork-

The birder who discovers a concentration of shorebirds can usually add to the day's bird list by setting up a spotting scope and studying them carefully.

ers are coming into a prearranged headquarters, often a restaurant or local hotel. There they compile their lists of observations for the day. This is the first opportunity they have of seeing how well their group has done for the year. Will the total species and individuals observed equal those of the preceding year? What new species might have turned up during this long day in the field? Will their records include as many birds as found by the census takers who annually work the nearby wildlife refuge or the area on the other side of the city? These are the questions on the bird watchers' minds as the leader calls off the names of the birds and their numbers are recorded.

There is purpose and a growing importance to this annual census of winter birds. By studying the records sent into the National Audubon Society from all corners of the country, ornithologists have been able to map in detail the advancing populations of imported house sparrows and starlings as they spread across the continent. Likewise, they have been able to follow the expanding range of the house finch, cattle egret, double-crested cormorant, and others. Fluctuations in mallards, black ducks, and other waterfowl have been revealed by the Christmas bird census. So have changes in populations of birds of prey such as Cooper's hawks and sharp-shinned hawks, whose numbers have dipped

Be a Conservationist

In the early 1970s, citizens of Florida who keep careful watch on the bird life of that state were appalled to find that the route for an important interstate highway planned in southern Florida would destroy a towering pine tree that for many years had worn an eagle nest in its crown. The southern bald eagle, perched as it is on the official list of rare and endangered species, is a matter of much public concern. It is confronted by a multitude of threats wherever it still lives. Since European man first began to settle the North American continent, the eagles have been declining. First this was from destruction of habitat as forests were cut and waters polluted. But the eagles began vanishing with even greater speed following World War II. In those years the chlorinated hydrocarbons, the most famous of which is DDT, came into widespread use across the country. It was not known then that, in addition to killing insects, these chemicals would destroy birds by causing them to lay eggs with shells so thin they broke in the nest. Eagles, being at the top of their food chains, accumulated stores of DDE, a DDT metabolite, in their fat and became major victims of this modern development. In addition, irresponsible gunners continued to shoot eagles. Some eagles were electrocuted by high-power lines; some young and inexperienced birds were killed on the highways; others were caught in traps set for coyotes and bobcats. All these things together have taken their toll of the bald eagle and made the fate of any nesting pair,

such as those in the path of the Florida highway, a matter of grave concern.

It might seem that when the highway planners set their gigantic machinery in motion, nothing could be done to alter the route. People in Florida, however, were quick to prove that this is not so. They appealed the case of the threatened pair of eagles to the appropriate authorities. The happy result was that a section of the highway was rerouted, and for the first time, perhaps, in the country's history a major interstate highway made a long sweeping curve around a bird's nest.

This is the kind of decision in which concerned conservationists everywhere can play a role. In the unceasing effort to save America's wildlife and the wildlife habitats, everyone can help and everyone's influence counts.

Bird watchers should be active conservationists seeking to preserve wildlife and their various environments for future generations. There is a multitude of ways in which this can be accomplished. Downstream from Cincinnati, astride the Ohio-Indiana border, lies a 2500-acre area of rich riverbottom farmland known as the Oxbow where there is a prehistoric oxbow lake. Local birders have long known that hundreds of migrating ducks, shorebirds, and wading birds stop here and store up energy to complete their journeys. It is the most important single wetland area remaining in the central Ohio Valley, and when local conservationists learned of plans to turn the area into a port authority for river barge

The osprey, sometimes called fish hawk, is one of the world's most widely distributed birds. Once disappearing, it began to recover following a ban on the insecticide DDT. *William C. Krantz, U.S. Fish and Wildlife Service.*

commerce, they organized Oxbow, Inc., and began collecting money through birdathons and other sources. Then they began buying up key parcels of land within the area as it came on the market. They signed conservation easements with landowners who didn't want to sell. The port authority plan was dropped. Because of the fast action of these conservationists, the Oxbow area was permanently reserved for wildlife.

One major example still fresh in the memories of conservationists is the case of the Cross Florida Barge Canal. By destroying much of the magnificent wooded valley of the Oklawaha River in central Florida the water developers would have created a large canal. Sacrificed forever, in the process, would have been thousands of acres of natural habitat occupied by birds and other wild creatures.

The plans for this multimillion-dollar canal drew opposition from across the country. Conservationists in every state wrote their congressmen and contributed their dollars to the fight to save the Oklawaha. The bulldozers ground on.

Finally, in January 1971, because of an Executive Order from the office of the President in Washington, D.C., these bulldozers stopped and the Cross-Florida Barge Canal was halted. Without the determined effort of conservationists the Oklawaha Valley would have been destroyed forever.

Farther south in the same state, conservationists succeeded in bringing to a halt the plans for a giant jet port which would have threatened by pollution and human intrusion the unique Everglades. Again it was the combined efforts of concerned people making their opinions known in high places that stopped the project.

Water development plans, such as dams, destroy whole ecosystems. In the 1960s, there was such a plan for the Buffalo River in Arkansas. Buried beneath the waters would have been scenic hill country, which has since become a national recreation area. It was saved because of the efforts again of conservationists who chose to be activists.

Among the major forces threatening what remains of the wildlife habitat today are mismanagement of forests including our national forests, wetland drainage, misuse of recreational vehicles, highways, dams, strip mining, stream channelization, and commercial and housing developments that may be poorly planned. Fortunately, citizens can be heard on questions concerning environmental protection.

Budding conservationists should not gain the impression that all their actions must be negative. Efforts to enlarge park systems, including community, city, and county parks, can be important in creating and preserving wildlife habitat. Often these efforts call for widespread public support, and concerned bird watchers can lend their weight. Local nature centers almost always need new members and volunteers. Bird clubs can become important forces in their own communities as they broaden their scope and enter the conservation arena. A number of national conservation organizations deserve support, and bird watchers should try to maintain membership in one or more of these groups. While national conservation organizations may have the greatest impact with Congress, local groups hold high promise for grassroots accomplishments.

When citizens around the San Francisco Bay National Wildlife Refuge understood that the refuge needed to be 20,000 acres larger to save a vital ecosystem, they organized the Citizens Committee to Complete the Refuge. All around the Bay, people began to hear the refuge story. There were bumper stickers, lapel buttons, petitions, public service messages on radio and television, letter writing, fund raising, and marshalling of scientific facts supporting the cause. Four hundred and fifty people attended a local meeting with the area's congressman. The result was a success story—Congress added 20,000 vital acres to the refuge.

In these years of environmental concern, many newspapers frequently carry stories telling of new developments in the out of doors, new threats to the environment both locally and nationally. The alert bird watcher/conservationist responds by writing brief thoughtful letters to governors, congressmen, and others who might be influential.

There is satisfaction in being an active conservationist. This broadens the birder's world and does something in return for the wildlife that we enjoy around our homes, gardens, farms, cities, and public lands.

Precautions for Bird Watchers

Human presence in a bird's nesting territory can bring stress to the bird and sometimes lead to tragedies. The first responsibility must be to the bird. Its welfare is more important than a visitor's life list, photographic collection, or curiosity. People frequently cause nesting birds more harm than they might have intended. This can grow from a lack of understanding of the bird and its nature, and the safe rule is to stay well away from the nest or young of birds if you do not know how they might react to human presence.

Especially critical is the time before the eggs hatch. Approaching the nest too closely or touching nest or eggs can cause the adults to abandon. Such invasion may also chill the eggs or leave young or eggs unguarded long enough to permit predators to slip in and take them.

Areas occupied by ground nesting colonial birds should not be invaded beyond the edge of the colony. There is always the danger of stepping on nests. The stress of human presence among such nesting birds as pelicans, gulls, shearwaters, terns, petrels, and boobies can

Newly hatched birds such as this tricolored heron chick quickly die in the scorching sun if the parent birds are kept from the nest.

The brown booby and her fluffy white chick are residents of a protected island within the Hawaiian Islands National Wildlife Refuge.

increase predation, damage, and abandonment. It is a good rule to cut any visit to an active bird nest as short as possible.

There was a time, years ago, when naturalists collected birds and eggs as evidence of their observations. But times have changed and so have laws. No longer is it legal to molest most birds or their eggs. Present-day bird watchers are concerned for the welfare of the birds and take great care to disturb them as little as possible.

Even where there are no bird nests in sight, invaders can cause trouble for the wildlife of some areas. Avoid prolonged exploration of wildlife marshes during the courting and nesting seasons. Invaders in these critical times may discourage birds that might otherwise establish nesting territories. The margins of marshes are particularly sensitive and susceptible to damage,

A White ibis on its nest of sticks in a Florida wildlife refuge.

and the vegetation is vitally important to the area ecology.

For their own safety, bird watchers do well to avoid public hunting areas during the open season, except on those days, such as Sundays or holidays, when the areas may be closed to gunning. License fees paid by sportsmen are, inci-dentally, often the source of funds for purchasing and paying for such fish and game areas.

Bird watchers who want to go on private land should first obtain permission, then remember to close gates, drop no litter, and not walk through growing crops or otherwise damage property on which they are guests.

Hazards of Bird Watching

Although bird watching has been billed as an innocent hobby for elderly ladies, which it can be, any field activity, whether the pursuit of birds, butterflies, or elephants, sometimes brings people into hazardous situations. Those who elect to band eagles, climb the highest trees, and scale the faces of cliffs to reach the eyries know the hazards of their choice. But seemingly mundane bird-watching trips can sometimes lead to unexpected problems also.

More than one bird watcher has lost himself in the deep forest, and this can be a serious dilemma, particularly in a wilderness area. Those inclined to penetrate remote regions should go well equipped and preferably in the company of someone well acquainted with the region. Carry maps, compass, matches, and an emergency food bar or two. A whistle for signaling friends is not a bad idea if used only for emergencies. In the eastern part of the nation, a downstream hike will almost invariably bring a person to road, railroad, or town eventually. In some western areas, the hike may be longer and it could lead into a box canyon. Panic is a real enemy. The best plan is to sit down and think the situation through, and if darkness comes, to settle down for the night. The person who remains calm can survive for days—or weeks—in the wilderness.

Proper clothing plays a major role in both comfort and protection in the outdoors. Good walking shoes that provide comfort, support, and offer security against slipping on smooth surfaces, are especially important.

Too much sun is a hazard. Long sleeves and a hat with a wide brim are good protection. Trousers are better than shorts, not just as protection from the sun, but also to guard against briars and bushes.

For some people, poison ivy, poison sumac, and poison oak are real outdoor hazards, and the best protection is learning to recognize these plants in time to avoid them.

As protection against ticks, wear light-colored clothing on which these little pests become visible, tuck your trousers into your boots, and inspect for ticks each evening.

A good mosquito repellent has a place in your day pack or pocket.

Snakes? The level of fear of these reptiles varies with individuals. Most of us won't see half a dozen snakes—even non-venomous ones—in a season. There are some precautions, however, that make good sense. Most snakebites are on the hands or lower parts of the arms and legs. Boots and loose-fitting trousers will help protect legs. If I were a snake sunning myself on a rocky ledge and the hand of a climbing human suddenly descended on me, I'd bite it in self-protection. Or if I were resting in the shade of a log and a boot came down upon my back, I'd employ my only defense. If I were a water moccasin living in a southern swamp on a summer day, I would not welcome a stranger who paused to sit on the stump where I customarily coiled up to take the sun.

The fact remains that, most of the time in most places, the possibility of seeing a snake is slender and should not be allowed to interfere with a day of birding. For those who learn to identify the common snakes, sighting one of these reptiles adds interest to a trip afield. In case of a bite by a venomous snake, the victim should be kept quiet and get medical attention as quickly as possible.

Lyme Disease

Lyme disease has been on the rise in recent times. Reported cases in humans increased from about 500 in 1982 to more than 9,300 a decade later. The danger of contracting this tick-borne disease, and the complications it can bring, depends on the part of the country, the season, and the care taken to prevent tick bites.

This disease, more prevalent in some sections of the country than in others, is transmitted to people and dogs by various species of ticks. This does not mean that every tick bite causes Lyme disease—even if the offending tick is infected with the spirochete. Chances are that you can avoid the disease if you remove the tick early enough.

According to the Lyme Disease Foundation, Inc., perhaps ninety percent of Lyme disease cases come from bites by ticks in the nymph stage, and at this stage in a tick's life cycle it is pinhead sized and difficult to see.

Before going into the field in tick seasons, especially in summer, use a good insect repellent applied to the clothing around your legs. Tuck pants legs into boots or socks.

If you find an imbedded tick, remove it as soon as possible. The longer it is there, the greater the possibility that it will infect its host. Most of my life I've heard that a tick can be removed by touching it with a lighted match or covering it with fingernail polish. These don't work well and may actually increase the risk of infection. The more common advice is to use a pair of tweezers to extract the little pest, then apply a disinfectant.

If Lyme disease does show up, it appears from a few days to a month after the bite and usually shows a red rash around the bite area. It is time to get immediate medical treatment.

Whether Lyme disease is known to be prevalent in the area or not, it is a good plan in season to inspect for ticks at the end of the day or even before.

Ways to Help Birds

1. Maintain bird feeders.

2. Build and erect birdhouses.

3. Put bells on your cats, and keep dogs under control.

4. Use discarded Christmas trees for wildlife shelters.

5. Avoid mowing fields where birds are nesting.

6. Install predator guards on nest box poles and feeding stations.

7. Offer nesting materials for birds.

8. Leave sunflower, millet, sorghum, corn, standing along field edges.

9. Plant decorative shrubs that produce bird foods.

10. Place hawk and owl silhouettes on picture windows to prevent crashes.

11. Do not burn fields during nesting seasons.

12. Protect all hawks and owls.

13. Do not approach active bird nests.

14. Maintain a birdbath.

15. Pick up plastic, monofilament fishing line and other litter in which birds might become entangled.

16. Purchase a migratory waterfowl stamp annually.

17. On your state income tax form, mark the check-off for non-game wildlife.

18. Join a conservation organization.

19. Vote "yes" on bond issues to provide more parks and green space.

20. Urge legislators to protect wilderness and wetlands against development.

III

SOME COMMON BIRDS

The following are introductions to birds that are often seen. Many of these are favorites around our homes and gardens.

Tufted Titmouse

Parus bicolor

A grayish bird with a prominent crest, the tufted titmouse is about the size of a house sparrow. It is often seen at the bird feeder with the chickadees. Sunflower seeds attract the titmouse in winter. It comes to the feeder, chooses a seed, and flies with it to a nearby tree. There the titmouse anchors the seed against the limb with its feet and pecks at it until it opens. The tufted titmouse, which is found in the eastern half of the United States, is common in the deciduous forest, where it is usually found, not in the treetops, but in the lower branches. Like the chickadee, it is a cavity nester, and its nest is usually ten to thirty feet from the ground. It packs leaves, mosses, hair, and feathers into its nesting cavity, and there the female deposits five to eight eggs, white and spotted with reddish brown. The titmouse does not migrate. If you do your birding in western states, you will encounter the plain titmouse instead, and if you live in Texas you may know the black-crested titmouse. All these cousins are somewhat similar in appearance as well as in the calls and songs they practice.

American Robin

Turdus migratorius

Robins are everybody's birds. They are seen from coast to coast and are found north into the Arctic tundra. They commonly move south for the winter, sometimes congregating in large flocks. The male's head is blackish, the wings, back, and tail gray, and the breast a bright reddish brown. The female is somewhat duller in color. Young robins, sometimes seen in the yard when first out of the nest, have streaked or spotted markings on their underparts. The robin is a mighty worm eater. It is often found running across the moist yard from one feeding spot to the next, cocking its head to see better, alert to catch the first worm that comes far enough out of its burrow to be available. The young are raised in a well-built nest, a combination of weeds, strings, and grass, all bound together by a smooth mud lining. The nest may be placed in the fork of a tree or under the roof of a porch. The three or four pale blue eggs take twelve or thirteen days to hatch, and for the next two weeks, until their young are ready to leave the nest, the parent robins are constantly busy finding food for them and delivering it to the nest.

Eastern Bluebird

Sialia sialis

In various seasons, the eastern bluebird is found from southern Canada to the Gulf Coast, and wherever it is found it is welcome. Its summer foods include beetles, grasshoppers, and other insects often caught in mid-air. The male, wearing his brilliant blue colors on back, wings, and tail, is the flashy member of the bluebird family. His mate is colored somewhat duller, wearing more gray and less blue on her back. The young are heavily spotted but already show signs of blue on tail and wings. Their natural nesting place is in a hollow limb. These cavity nesters that make their nests in hollow trees or posts readily accept the invitation to raise their families in nest boxes. The eggs are three to seven in number and pale bluish or almost white in color. Incubation requires about twelve days and is done mostly by the female. In about fifteen days, the young bluebirds are out of the nest. The female is then ready to start a second brood. Some pairs even raise a third family ahead of fall. In late summer, where you see one bluebird you may see several because the family group stays together in a loose flock, sometimes through the winter. North America has two other species of bluebirds, the western bluebird, which has a blue throat, and its cousin the mountain bluebird, which, unlike the others, has no rust coloring on its blue-gray breast.

Northern Mockingbird

Mimus polyglottos

Superb songster and a bit of a clown, the mockingbird may be the most visible bird around any yard or garden where it establishes its home. Not content to sing its own notes, it mimics the songs of its neighbors and continues to practice them in an ever-changing medley, night and day. About the size of a robin, the mockingbird is, however, somewhat more slender and equipped with a longer tail. It is light gray above, dark gray on the wings. As the mockingbird flies across the yard, its flashing white wing and tail patches provide ready identification marks. Its nest is a bulky affair built at low elevation in thick brush. In this structure the female lays four to six eggs, all shaded in pale blue-green and heavily spotted with brown.

Northern Cardinal

Cardinalis cardinalis

The flashing red cardinal is well known year-round wherever it lives. The male's bright red feathering, pointed crest, and black throat make it easily identified. The female likewise has a crest, but her coloring is duller. These welcome birds are common residents around home gardens and shrubbery, adding an especially bright touch to the winter landscape when their brilliant colors stand out boldly against the snow. Cardinals are regular guests at the bird feeder and are especially fond of sunflower seed, which they crack easily with their thick bills. Their nest, which may be fairly close to the ground in a thick bush or evergreen tree, is neatly fashioned from weeds and grasses, then lined with rootlets and other fine materials. There are usually three or four eggs, speckled gray or lilac on a white background.

Common Flicker

Colaptes auratus

A large flashy woodpecker and easily recognized, the flicker is a common resident in city and rural areas alike. It is about the size of a blue jay. The flicker commonly seen in the eastern half of the country is the yellow-shafted flicker, replaced in the West by the red-shafted flicker, and in the Southwest, where the giant saguaro cactus grows, by the gilded flicker. All three are similar in size and coloring, with minor differences known to the serious bird student. The yellow-shafted flicker is known in flight by the golden colors of its flashing wings and the large white tail patch. Frequently, the flicker may be observed hopping about in the front yard, searching for insects, particularly ants. For its nest the flicker chisels out a cavity in the trunk or limb of a tree. Here the female deposits seven or eight glossy white eggs.

House Wren

Troglodytes aedon

The house wren, sometimes called jenny wren, tail pointing skyward, bubbling over with song, is a favorite of all who have this common little bird around their homes and yards. In contrast to some of our wild birds, this little wren seems to have prospered by man's presence. Few other birds seem as willing as the house wren to accept man's hospitality. House wrens have been known to nest in old straw hats or the pockets of overalls left hanging in garage or shed. Into their bulky nest go five to nine pinkish white eggs with little reddish brown spots. About September, after the young wrens are raised and on their own, the house wrens depart to spend the winter along the Gulf Coast. But as surely as April comes again they return, announcing their arrival with a welcome song.

Mourning Dove

Zenaida macroura

The mourning dove is a speedy flier that travels on whistling wings. Somewhat larger than a robin, the mourning dove is tinted in soft grays and browns, its bill black, feet reddish. In the sunlight, parts of its plumage flash iridescent colors. Almost certainly there are more mourning doves in the country today than there were in prehistoric times. This bird has prospered with the coming of man. It feeds in his grain fields and nests in the shrubbery around both city homes and farm buildings. It comes to the winter feeding station especially when offered small grain scattered on the ground. The nest is a flimsy platform of flat twigs loosely arranged on a horizontal branch, and in it the female places two white eggs. The young are fed by regurgitation.

Blue Jay

Cyanocitta cristata

There is nothing quiet and well mannered about the blue jay. This large dashing bird of forest and garden has a loud and unmusical call. On occasion it will mimic the calls of other birds. The blue jay has bright blue colors mixed with white areas on back, wings, and tail and is lighter on its underparts. It wears a prominent crest on its head. Males and females look alike and are somewhat larger than the robin. There is little chance of confusing them with other birds. The nest of blue jays is constructed of twigs, rootlets, and weed stalks all brought together in a bulky structure and formed into a neat cup in the center. It is usually placed from ten to thirty feet above ground. There are three to six eggs, pale gray-green in color and heavily spotted with brown and gray. Some people dislike the blue jay for its habit of robbing the nests of other birds. But this has been done for centuries, and to the blue jay it is neither right nor wrong. Blue jays are common winter visitors at the feeder, frequently arriving in pairs. Their favorite wild foods at this season include acorns and beechnuts, but at the feeder they are quick to accept sunflower seeds and peanuts. The blue jay is a bold and colorful bird, and most bird watchers welcome him to their yards and gardens.

Black-capped Chickadee

Parus atricapillus

Seven species of chickadees are widely distributed through the United States and Canada, and all have black bibs and dark, usually black, caps. The best known of the clan is the four-inch-long black-capped chickadee. This little bird is common around winter feeders and particularly welcome because of its acrobatic talents. It hangs upside down on the suet feeder and swings with confidence on the wind-buffeted maple twigs. Winter and summer the chickadee is likely to be seen around gardens and woodlands. Its summer food leans heavily to insects, but during winter includes much vegetable matter. Nests of the chickadee are normally built in hollow limbs, frequently those carved out by woodpeckers. Into these home-sites the chickadee carries an assortment of leaves, moss, and grass. It lines its nest with hair, feathers, and sometimes fur, to provide a resting place for from four to eight eggs, which are white, but spotted with chestnut and gray.

Red-winged Blackbird

Agelaius phoeniceus

The red-winged blackbird, known from coast to coast, comes north in early spring. The males arrive well ahead of the females and travel in large flocks over the wetlands. Each male defends his own territory. He perches on the brown stems of last year's cattails and the willow branches singing his gurgling, bubbly song while his wings fluff out. This is his announcement to the world that his territory is established. When the females arrive, the male attempts to attract a mate to this territory. The mated pair builds a nest that is a tightly constructed grass cup, sometimes braced in the cattails above the water, sometimes placed in the meadow. There the female lays three to five eggs, which are pale blue and streaked with purple or black. She incubates her eggs for ten to fourteen days. The male is easily recognized for his over-all black coloring, sometimes with a bluish cast, and brilliant scarlet shoulder patches, which are usually lined with a band of buff or white. His mate is much more drab in coloring, brownish and heavily streaked. By late summer the redwings are gathering in giant flocks along with grackles, cowbirds, and starlings. Except for those farmers whose grain they may destroy, most people like redwings and enjoy seeing them beside ponds and over the marshes. In recent times they have even adapted to nesting in hay fields. They are a colorful part of the bird world and a special favorite when they announce the return of spring.

Downy Woodpecker

Picoides pubescens

The downy woodpecker, about the size of a house sparrow, is common around homes and gardens. It comes readily to bird feeders, especially where suet is available. There is only one other bird that it is likely to be confused with, a larger cousin, the hairy woodpecker. They are similarly marked in black and white with rows of heavy white spots on the wings. Except for one small area on the outer tail feathers, the downy and hairy woodpeckers show no difference in color patterns. On these white outer tail feathers the downy woodpecker has barred markings, the hairy woodpecker no markings. The male, but not the female, has a red spot on the back of its head. They are recognized quickly by their habits. Woodpecker-fashion, the downy clings to trees with its sharp claws,

One bird likely to be confused with the more common downy woodpecker is the slightly larger hairy woodpecker shown here feeding on seeds of the staghorn sumac. The bill of the hairy woodpecker is noticeably thicker. *Karl H. Maslowski.*

bracing itself with the pointed feathers at the end of its tail. There it hops about searching for insects. The downy woodpecker is a permanent resident. It builds its nest in a cavity in a tree. There are three to five glossy white eggs.

Gray Catbird

Dumetella carolinensis

The catbird, named for its catlike call, is easily recognized by its dark gray color. It is smaller than a robin, has a long tail and a black cap, and its undertail coverts are rust-colored. It is often seen around thick shrubbery bordering yards and orchards. The catbird eats mostly insects and berries and flies south for the winter months. The nest of the catbird is large and bulky, built of twigs and lined with rootlets or grapevine bark. There the female lays three to five eggs, glossy, and deep blue-green in color. The catbird usually hides its nest in thickets and tangled shrubbery. It belongs to the same family of imitators as the mockingbird and brown thrasher. But the catbird's musical skills and ability to mimic its neighbors are limited as compared with the considerably larger mockingbird.

American Kestrel

Falco sparverius

Formerly called sparrow hawk, this robin-sized falcon, is often seen around open fields and along country roads. Its habit of hovering over open fields while hunting helps birders identify it. It is frequently seen perching on telephone lines or trees. The kestrel, particularly the male, is a beautifully colored bird. Its back is rust-colored, the head is a combination of rust, blue, black, and white, and the wings are bluish gray spotted with black. The females are somewhat duller in color. The food of this hawk is largely grasshoppers, mice, and other small rodents. Like all hawks, it is fully protected by law. During the summer months when they come north to nest and raise their young, they occupy cavities in trees or set up housekeeping in bird boxes. The eggs are four to eight in number, buff-colored, and heavily spotted with reddish brown.

Brown Thrasher

Toxostoma rufum

A favorite with all who come to know it, the brown thrasher lives east of the Rocky Mountains. It is a migrant, invading the northern states and southern Canada in summer to raise its young. The brown thrasher is about the size of a robin and has a much longer tail. Its tail, back, and wings are reddish brown with bold white crossbars on the wings. The light underparts are heavily streaked with black. The colors are similar to those of the wood thrush, but the wood thrush is a smaller bird with a much shorter tail. Another identifying mark that sets the thrasher apart from similar birds is its bright yellow eye. Brown thrashers are often found in the thickets along country lanes. The brown thrasher has its own song but will also mimic those of its wild neighbors. The nest is a bulky affair, fashioned of twigs and lined with rootlets and strips of grass. Ordinarily the nest is only a few feet above the ground. The three to six eggs are whitish, finely dotted with browns and grays.

Cedar Waxwing
Bombycilla cedrorum

Neat, trim, and well groomed, the cedar waxwing often travels in flocks and is a welcome addition to the bird-watcher's list. Olive gray, with darker gray on wings and tail, it wears a black mask edged in white and has black on its throat. Also distinguishing it is a high distinct crest. This and the somewhat larger Bohemian waxwing are the only birds you are likely to see with yellow-tipped outer tail feathers. These two species can be told apart by the undertail coverts, white on the cedar waxwing, rust-colored on the Bohemian. The Bohemian waxwing also wears white and yellow marks on its wings. Cedar waxwings are often seen in fruit trees. Flocks of them feed heavily on cedar berries, pokeberries, and Virginia creeper. They will also eat insects, sometimes catching them on the wing, as do the flycatchers. The nest of the cedar waxwing may be twelve to twenty feet from the ground and is constructed of weeds, twigs, and fibers. The blue-gray eggs, spotted with black, usually number three to six.

Ruby Throated Hummingbird
Archilochus colubris

Any bird watcher has a red-letter day when he finds the nest of the ruby-throated hummingbird. This minute, darting flier builds a small, lichen-covered, cup-shaped nest straddling a limb. Its two navy-bean-sized eggs must be incubated for fourteen days. Food for the ruby-throat is composed of tiny insects and nectar taken from flowers. Hummingbirds can be attracted to home gardens by growing nectar-producing flowers or by hanging hummingbird feeders filled with sugar water. The ruby-throated hummingbird is more likely to be confused with a large hawk moth than it is with another bird. The colors of the male are iridescent green on the head, back and wings with a brilliant ruby throat, and white underparts. The female is somewhat duller and lacks the red throat of her mate. In spite of their small size, ruby-throated hummingbirds, during their migration flights, take a five-hundred-mile nonstop trip across the Gulf of Mexico. This is the only hummingbird native to the eastern half of the country.

European Starling
Sturnus vulgaris

The starling is a stoutly proportioned bird with a long, sharp bill and a short tail. They are often seen in large flocks, sometimes mixed with other blackbirds—grackles, cowbirds, and red wings. Imported from Europe, the starling spread widely, creating new enemies, even among bird watchers. It is disliked not only because it damages farm crops but also because it takes over the living spaces that might otherwise go to native cavity-dwelling species. It is quick to claim possession of birdhouses, and it nests early in the season, often before native birds return to establish territories. The starling sometimes fools bird watchers by mimicking other species such as the bobwhite and wood pewee. But the starling is not all bad; in spring and summer it feeds heavily on insects. When it walks about our front yards, as it frequently does, it is usually searching for larvae among the grass roots. The nest of this alien is an assembly of grass, straw, twigs, and feathers. There are usually five to eight pale blue or whitish eggs. Incubation takes eleven to fourteen days, with both sexes taking turns on the nest.

American Goldfinch
Carduelis tristis

In summer the male goldfinch's lemon-yellow body, with black wings and forehead, is easily recognized as he swings from thistles and other flowering plants. His mate is not so brilliantly colored. Goldfinches are also often seen in winter, frequently eating seeds at feeding stations where they may go unrecognized. In these cold months both sexes wear dull grayish yellow colors. In winter they live in flocks. They are almost exclusively seed eaters. Another feature by which the goldfinches are known is their habit of flying, not in a straight line, but following an up-and-down path, singing in a pleasant high-pitched series of notes as they fly. Their nest is built in a small fork of a tree or shrub, where they fashion soft thistledown and other fine plant materials into a bulky cup. Here the female places four to six bluish white eggs, which she incubates for eleven to fourteen days with no help from the male.

Eastern Meadowlark
Sturnella magna

The meadowlark is the friend of country boys. Its melodious high-pitched song is heard from the hayfields, where its brilliant yellow under-parts add a flash of color to the summer scene. At first glance the eastern and western mead-owlarks, about robin-sized, are much alike. The underparts are a brilliant yellow. There is a bold black V or bib across the breast, and the feathers of the back are brownish and patterned with white and black. The outer tail feathers are white. The nest of the meadowlark is built in open fields, and it is a cup formed of grasses built on the ground. When her nest is finished, the female fashions the grasses over it into a canopy that helps to hide it. In this secret place she deposits three to seven eggs, whitish but spotted with brown and purple. Incubation takes fifteen to seventeen days, with male and female taking turns to keep the eggs warm. Insects make up about 99 percent of the diet, and it has a special fondness for cut worms, which helps qualify it as a friend of the farmer. The eastern meadowlark, *Sturnella magna,* has a western cousin, *Sturnella neglecta,* and their ranges overlap. They are best told apart by differences in their songs.

Baltimore Oriole
Icterus galbula

If you hear a loud cheerful summer song from the top of the elms or maple trees, watch for the brilliant black and orange of the oriole. Birds of this species are similar to the Bullock's oriole in the West, but there are differences in their plumages. The male oriole is one of the most beautiful birds on the summer scene. The head, neck, back, wings, and tail are mostly black. A brilliant orange marks the underparts, the outer tail feathers, and the rump. The bill is long and narrow. The female, wearing much duller colors, is mostly olive brownish in color. This oriole is an excellent nest builder, hanging its home in the forks of a twig near the end of a limb in a very tall tree. It is a gray pouch woven of fine hair, plant materials, and string. In this suspended bag, the female lays four to six eggs, grayish white and marked with streaks and spots of brown, black, and lavender. She handles the fourteen-day incubation period without any help from her mate, who becomes an ornament in the treetops filling the neighborhood with his loud, bold song. For winter the orioles migrate to Central and South America.

Killdeer

Charadrius vociferus

A robin-sized member of the shorebird family, the killdeer is easily recognized and is well known to farmers. It often lives in open pastures, cultivated fields, and golf courses, where it feeds mostly on insects. It has long legs and a short bill, moves nervously, and makes a lot of noise. As it flies away, it is likely to repeat a string of "*killdeer, killdeer*" calls, which give it its name. The upper parts of the killdeer are brownish gray. Especially visible as it flies are the brightly colored orange tail feathers banded with white and black. The underparts are white, and there are two prominent black bands across its neck and breast. If, in summer, you should come upon a killdeer that seems to have a broken wing and flutters ahead of you, tempting you to chase it, you are probably close to its nest or newly hatched young. As soon as it has lured you far enough from its eggs, the killdeer suddenly recovers and takes flight. The nest, no fancy structure, is a dish-shaped depression in the field. It may be lined with a few twigs or pebbles. There are usually four eggs, well camouflaged by spots and streaks of brown and black. Both sexes share in the twenty-four to twenty-six days of incubation. Its winters are spent from the southern part of the United States into Venezuela and Peru.

Yellow Warbler

Dendroica petechia

Across the United States and Canada the yellow warbler is a common summer resident. It is a small bird, much smaller than the house sparrow. Both the male and the female are bright yellow, but the male wears lines of reddish brown spots the length of its undersides. The back is a slightly duller olive drab. These birds commonly feed on beetles, caterpillars, weevils, and other insects. They may be observed in shrubbery around the home grounds, in orchards, or in the thickets along the edges of woodlands. The nest is a cuplike structure which the pair constructs two to twelve feet above ground in the fork of a small tree or bush. Normally it will hold three to five eggs, light gray or greenish in color and spotted with brown. For eleven days the female must incubate the eggs. Then both parents work through the daylight hours for about ten or eleven more days carrying food and feeding the young before the little warblers are able to fly. The cowbird often selects the nests of the yellow warbler for its own eggs. Then the yellow warbler may sacrifice its eggs along with that of the cowbird by building a floor over all of them and adding a new level to the nest. Several such false floors may be built into one yellow warbler's nest.

Green Heron

Butorides striatus

Fishermen and canoeists often encounter the green heron along quiet wooded streams and around ponds. When frightened or excited, this interesting bird elevates the shaggy crest on its head. At a distance or in poor light, the green heron seems to be generally grayish green in color. But a closer look reveals its yellow or orange legs, generally dark underparts, and a reddish brown neck. It spends its winters from

The tricolored heron is a common resident of salt-water marshes and swamps in southeastern states and around the Gulf Coast.

Florida and the southeastern states into Central America and the northern edge of Colombia. It nests northward to North Dakota and eastward to Nova Scotia. The nest of the green heron is found in low trees or thickets over water and is little more than a flimsy platform of sticks. The eggs, pale blue and numbering three to nine, are incubated for seventeen days. The parent birds are likely to carry grasshoppers, crickets, snakes, snails, fish, worms, and even mice to their young.

Mallard

Anas platyrhynchos

Best known of the wild ducks, the mallard is the ancestor of most domesticated varieties. It is a large duck, and the male in breeding plumage is brilliantly colored. He is known for his metallic-green head, white neck band, and rust-colored breast. On his wings he has a patch of blue with white borders. The female also has this wing mark but otherwise is much different in color from her mate. She is mottled and streaked with grayish browns, a color combination that helps her hide from predators while on the nest. The eggs are laid in ground-level nests, hidden in the grass and weeds, usually near water. They may number from six to fifteen and are greenish to gray brown. Incubation lasts twenty-six to twenty-eight days, all of it handled by the female, who is also responsible for rearing the young. In winter, the mallards migrate to open southern waters, where they can find food in shallow marshes and ponds. The summer diet ranges from mosquito larvae to the tender parts of aquatic plants. In autumn, they are quick to add grain, where available, to their diet.

Canada Goose
Branta canadensis

It is perhaps during migration flight that the large Canada goose is seen by most people. On a number of wildlife refuges, in recent years, management practices have drawn these birds from the skies in spectacular concentrations. Fall visitors to such places as Wheeler, Horicon, Ottawa, and Swan Lake national wildlife refuges sometimes view thousands of them. They are easily recognized. Male, female, and young are marked alike. The head and neck are black, and under the eye is a broad white "chin strap." The upper parts are brownish gray, the belly white. The nest is normally on grassy hummocks or small islands in marsh areas. The female is responsible for the twenty-eight days of incubation required to hatch the five dull white eggs. However, the gander is somewhere nearby standing guard, ready to charge out at any invading enemy. He may attack even large animals, man included. The size of the Canada goose varies with the subspecies, ranging from the little cackling goose weighing in at about five or six pounds to the giant Canada goose

which may weigh eighteen pounds or more. This giant subspecies is the one most likely to take up residence in and around centers of human population. It may loaf on golf courses and city ponds, and leave its droppings in backyards. But the geese remain popular, and city after city has encouraged them to become local permanent residents.

Rufous-sided Towhee
Pipilo erythrophthalmus

The towhee, slightly smaller than a robin, is a favorite of bird watchers. It is an occupant of the thick-growing brushy places along the edges of woodlands, hedgerows, and old farm lands reverting to trees. The head, neck, and upper parts of the male towhee are black, the sides chestnut-colored, and the underparts white. Flashing white shows on the tail as the towhee flies. The eye is bright red. Females do not have the black back but in its place wear grayish brown. The first hint that there is a towhee around may come when it is heard scratching chicken-fashion in the leaves. Its call is clear and loud, and it says "towhee." The towhee's nest is usually hidden at ground level in a thicket or clump of ferns. In this cuplike structure of leaves, bark, and rootlets, the female places four or five white eggs marked heavily with reddish brown. She alone is responsible for the incubation, which goes on for twelve or thirteen days. Then both parents bring food to the young. Much of this food consists of insects, but towhees also feed heavily on seeds and wild fruit.

Eastern Screech Owl
Otus asio

The screech owl comes in two colors, gray and red. Both color phases may be found in the same area, and in fact, a pair of screech owls may consist of a gray one and a red or rust-colored mate. These small owls are part of the night world and common around villages, farms, and woodlands, where they nest in tree cavities. They will also nest in bird boxes. They are known by their prominent ear tufts, which are easily seen and almost always visible when one gets close to a screech owl. They are heard more often than they are seen. These little owls are permanent residents. Mice are a major item in their diet.

Common Grackle
Quiscalus quiscula

This large black bird, the common grackle, has a long tail and a yellow eye and from a distance appears to be plain black. But close up its feathers take on a metallic sheen of iridescent greens, blues, or violets. The grackle is larger than the cowbird, redwing, and starling, with which it sometimes flocks. Its size and long tail serve to set it apart. The nest of the grackle is made of

The screech owl, known by its quavering nighttime call, can be attracted to birdhouses.

grasses and weeds and is a large cup-shaped structure sometimes strengthened with mud and often built in tall trees. There are usually three to seven eggs, which may vary from pale blue to whitish or gray, all heavily splotched with brown and black. Although the grackle feeds heavily on insects, it by no means limits its diet to pests. Sometimes it becomes a pest itself by feeding in farm crop fields and orchards. Grackles frequently walk about on lawns, where they search for insects hiding in the grass.

Dark-eyed Junco
Junco hyemalis

The junco, about the size of a house sparrow, is known far and wide to those who maintain winter bird-feeding stations. They nest to the north through the boreal forest and into the tundra. But in winter, they come south and are often seen in flocks in forests, weedy fields, and backyards where food is available. These are the seed eaters and can be attracted to bird feeders with small grain and sunflower seeds. Some dark-eyed juncos nest in the high mountain areas of the Appalachians at altitudes corresponding to the climate they would encounter in the Far North. The nest is woven of fine grasses, a cup, usually hidden in the woods at ground level. There are three to five white eggs, spotted with brown.

Song Sparrow
Melospiza melodia

One field mark by which bird watchers recognize the song sparrow is its heavily streaked breast with a large brown patch in the middle. This common bird of thickets and woodland borders is about the size of the house sparrow. It is reddish brown above. The nest of the song sparrow is on the ground or in a low bush

where cover is thick. It is fashioned from rootlets and grasses and lined with finer materials. Here the female places three to five eggs, greenish-colored and speckled with brown. She must incubate them for twelve to fourteen days. Male and female cooperate and gather food for the young during the nine or ten days needed for them to grow and leave the nest. Song sparrows eat seeds and other vegetable matter, but they also feed on insects.

Red-eyed Vireo
Vireo olivaceus

The red-eyed vireo, the size of a house sparrow, is believed by ornithologists to be the most abundant summer bird in the deciduous forest of the eastern part of the continent. But it is seldom noticed by most people. Its colors are plain, whitish below, olive drab above. Helping to identify it is a white eye stripe and a red eye. Much of the time it inhabits the treetops, and those who listen know it by its much repeated and sometimes monotonous warbling song. The nest is a cup of soft fibrous materials built by the female, in a forked limb from five to thirty feet above the ground. The female needs twelve to fourteen days to incubate the three or four eggs, which are white and lightly spotted with reddish brown. The male joins the female and helps in carrying food to the young for ten or twelve days until they leave the nest. Their meals consist of insects, varied now and then with a helping of wild fruit.

Wood Duck
Aix sponsa

The male wood duck in his spring plumage is among North America's most colorful birds. You will recognize him by his rainbow colors, the slicked back crest on his head, and often by his plaintive calls as he flies along the wooded stream where you are fishing or canoeing.

The wood duck's natural nest site is a hollow tree or limb beside a stream or woodland pond, or maybe half a mile or more from water if this is the best it can do.

After a month or so of incubating nine to twelve eggs, the female sees her ducklings hatch. They are ready to leave the nest as soon as they are dry. Waiting on the water below, she calls to them, urging them out of the safety of their nest cavity into the daylight. Using their sharp claws, the newly hatched ducklings climb up the inside of the nest cavity, stick their heads out, then launch themselves, one at a time, in a free fall that tumbles them, sometimes thirty or forty feet, to the ground or water below.

Earlier in this century the wood duck was threatened with extinction because drainage and timbering destroyed their habitat and gunners overshot them. But new restrictions saved them from the gun while conservationists, especially hunters and owners of wetlands, began building thousands of nest boxes for them. The result is an outstanding success story; wood ducks are abundant again, and birders add them to their lists of wetland birds with little trouble. Furthermore, anyone can help the wood duck by erecting more homes for this favorite bird. See page 114 for directions for building wood-duck boxes.

Great Blue Heron
Ardea herodias

This is the towering bluish-gray bird that, back home in my youth, we called "crane." It stands some three feet high, and close up the observer can see the light color of the head, a dark stripe over the eye, and dark plumes on the breeding male's head. We often see a great blue heron standing motionless in the edge of the creek or pond on those spindly stiltlike legs until a hapless fish swims within reach. Then, that long heron neck snakes out and there is no escape for the fish. Or we watch it lift off, on wings spreading across seven feet of air from tip to tip, and draw itself across the sky, with its long legs stretched out straight behind it.

The heron's nest is usually in the top of a towering tree surrounded by a dozen or more nests of other pairs. Both male and female incubate the three to seven eggs for about twenty-eight days. For the next two months or more the young must stay in the nest until strong enough to fly. The great blue heron is found over much of the continent.

White-throated Sparrow
Zonotrichia albicollis

Across the Midwest, East, and South, birders who maintain winter feeding stations often see this sparrow feeding on seeds at ground level. The white-throated sparrow favors brushy areas and comes most often to ground-level feeding stations located near good escape cover. It is recognized by white stripes on the head, white throat, and yellow spots in front of the eyes. This sparrow is sometimes confused with the white-crowned sparrow which is about the same size.

The white-throated sparrow moves north in late spring and spends the summer nesting season across much of Canada. The nest, hidden in the brush on or close to the ground, is shaped of grass, twigs, moss, and bark. Here the female lays three to five eggs which she must incubate for nearly two weeks before her young chicks hatch.

House Sparrow
Passer domesticus

Nearly everyone knows the house sparrow, but few admire it. In addition to being drab in color and unskilled as a vocalist, the house sparrow sometimes dominates bird feeders as well as nest boxes erected for martins and bluebirds. Or it may build its bulky nest of grass, tissues, string, and straw under rafters of homes and barns as well as city buildings, shopping malls, and fast-food emporia. Because it flocks to fields and grain storage areas, it has few friends among farmers. But, unaware that it is an outcast, the house sparrow crowds into all available space and is a year-round resident in almost every part of the country. It is drab in color, noisy and carefree about where it leaves its droppings. The house sparrow thrives in villages, cities, and around farms.

This bird is not a true American sparrow but a finch brought here from Europe. Sometimes called English sparrow, it flourishes today over most of the world because well-meaning, but ill-informed, people transplanted it widely.

Brown-headed Cowbird

Molothrus ater

Across much of the country birders are likely to see cowbirds in some season. If these small blackbirds had been officially named earlier, they might be called buffalo birds because they originally associated with bison. When domestic cattle replaced the bison herds, the birds readily adjusted. Cowbirds.

Male cowbirds are easily identified by their iridescent plumage and the dark brown coloring of the head. The females are grayish brown with streaked undersides.

The cowbird is a highly successful parasite; it enlists the help of its neighbors to raise its young. In early morning, the female slips through the bushes, depositing her eggs in the nests of birds of similar or smaller size. Some other birds parasitize the nests of neighbors, but among American birds the cowbird alone makes no effort to incubate its eggs. The female cowbird may make room for her own eggs by carrying off those of her hosts. Some of its victims,

including robins and catbirds, recognize the cowbird egg as an intruder and toss it out, while the yellow warbler builds a new floor over it and starts producing a new set of eggs. But some two hundred other species are known to have incubated the eggs of cowbirds along with, or instead of, their own.

But who are we to sit in judgment? The cowbird does not know that its carefree approach to home and family values offends some people. Evolution handed it a system that works—at least for cowbirds.

White-breasted Nuthatch

Sitta carolinensis

Winter or summer, one of my favorite birds is the white-breasted nuthatch. I often hear its loud nasal call before I see it. It is bluish-gray above with a dark cap and white face and underparts. It makes its living extracting insects from beneath the bark of forest trees as it climbs up or down and around the trunks.

Originally a forest bird, the nuthatch adapted to the presence of people with their shade trees and sunflower seed offerings.

The red-breasted nuthatch is smaller; it has reddish or rust coloring on the underside, a heavy black line through the eye, and a different call.

Black-billed Magpie

Pica pica

If you live in the western states, north into western Canada or Alaska, chances are good that you know magpies. These interesting neighbors are often seen around thickets, especially along creeks, where they live in small flocks except during the breeding season. They are easily recognized by their long tails and flashy black and white markings.

Magpies, which belong to the crow and jay

Black-billed magpie, known by its long tail and flashing white wing patches, is common along streams and in open fields in western states.

clan, commonly mate for life, or as long as the match is successful in producing young magpies. If they fail repeatedly, the pair may give up and separate.

The nest, which they often repair and use year after year, is a bulky domed structure built of sticks in a low tree. It is equipped with a mud cup lined with soft plant materials. Its dome offers predator protection, especially at night when owls are abroad. A slightly smaller relative, the yellow-billed magpie, lives in California.

Wild Turkey

Meleagris gallopavo

If, in these troubled times, we need a wildlife success story to buoy our spirits, the wild turkey is a prime candidate. As a boy, prior to World War II, I had never seen a turkey in the wild, because we had no wild turkeys left in Ohio, or in many other states. We read of pioneers taking these giant birds for dinner in whatever numbers they needed. But cutting the hardwood forests, plus overshooting, eliminated the turkeys through much of their native range.

Following World War II, with forests returning, state wildlife biologists began transplanting wild turkeys back to their historic range.

Starting in the early 1950's, Ohio went from no wild turkeys to vigorous populations throughout much of the state, and the same was true in other states. We now watch from the window of our farmhouse as a line of turkeys crosses the hillside meadow passing from one woods to another. And we hear the gobblers in spring when they call from the woods.

The hen turkey makes her nest on the ground, usually in the woods and often beside a fallen log or brush pile. Here she deposits a dozen or so eggs which she must incubate for twenty-eight days before leading her chicks off to begin learning how to support themselves, while watching for the approach of hawk, owl, fox, dog, or human.

Turkey Vulture

Cathartes aura

The turkey vulture is a hang glider, so skilled at riding the thermals that it seldom has to flap its wings. Usually you see the vulture at a distance, either on the wing or perched in a dead tree. Seen from below, as it flies, it shows black on the lead portions of the wings and a silvery gray on the flight feathers. The only bird likely to be confused with the turkey vulture is the black vulture. But the black vulture has a short tail and, when soaring, holds its wings almost level instead of in the shallow V formed by the turkey vulture's wings. Both have naked heads, black in the case of the black vulture, red in the adult turkey vulture. The turkey vulture has a much wider range and is seen from coast to coast and from southern Canada south into Mexico. The black vulture is a more southern species.

Vultures are primarily carrion eaters but sometimes kill small mammals, birds, and reptiles.

Normally turkey vultures lay two eggs, and a hollow log in a woodland thicket is a favorite site.

Eastern Phoebe

Sayornis phoebe

When the phoebes, perhaps the best known birds in the flycatcher family, return in early spring, they are always welcome. They come announcing their name in gentle tones—*Phoebe, Phoebe.* As the weather warms, and the flying insects on which they feed begin to hatch, the phoebes settle into their territories and begin gathering mud and moss to build the cup-shaped nests which they plaster to the side of a building beneath the eaves. Those that build their nests in woodlands sometimes attach them to rock ledges. There, on a soft lining of moss and hair, the female deposits four or five white eggs and begins incubating them.

Phoebes come in three species and the one you see depends on where you are. They are known for their trait of pumping the tail downward after they come to a perch. The plainest of the group is the eastern phoebe, a dull-gray, olive-green flycatcher, which has no distinguishing marks such as wing bars or eye rings. It is known in various seasons throughout the eastern United States and much of Canada. Say's Phoebe is a western bird with a rust-colored belly. The black phoebe, known by its black breast and white belly, is a bird of the Southwest.

John James Audubon gave this bird a historic distinction. His writings tell us that he attached a silver thread to the leg of a phoebe on a farm in Pennsylvania. The marked bird returned the following spring. This is believed to be the first time a bird was banded.

Whip-poor-will

Caprimulgus vociferus

Some years ago, I lay awake counting the calls of a whip-poor-will in the woods behind the house until the number exceeded one thousand calls, and I drifted off to sleep. That is by no means a record. This bird of the night, seldom seen but often heard, is found in summer in the eastern part of the United States north into Canada and in parts of the Southwest.

The whip-poor-will is a member of the nightjar or goatsucker family. They have wide mouths with which they net flying insects on the wing. The whip-poor-will's somewhat larger cousin, the chuck-will's-widow, is a bird of the Southeast that nests northward into southern Illinois, Indiana, and Ohio. It too is said to be named for its call, but it sounds to me as though it is calling, not *chuck-will's-widow* but *cluck-weddle-weddle, cluck-weddle-weddle.* Perhaps this is a fine distinction. One of my neighbors says the chuck-will's-widow sounds like a whip-poor-will with a sore throat.

In western states the family member is the poorwill, noted for its own call, but also known among scientists as the bird that sometimes hibernates because it may stay the winter, immobile and camouflaged, against a rock wall.

Another relative, the nighthawk, is common across much of Canada and the United States. It is often seen at dusk as it feeds over open fields. It has a loud nasal call and a large white spot on the underside of each wing.

House Finch

Carpodacus mexicanus

If in recent years you have noticed growing numbers of a reddish-tinged sparrow at your feeders, or in your yard in summer, you are probably seeing house finches. This is a western species, and there is an interesting story behind their invasion and spread through the East.

When dealers in caged birds decided that this colorful little bird with the sweet song could be a money maker, they began shipping them east and selling them. They called them Hollywood finches, and the trade continued until the U.S. Fish and Wildlife Service law enforcement agents moved in to shut down this illegal trade in wildlife. New York dealers, kind-hearted bird lovers that they were, took their house finch cages to the back doors of their shops and turned their little imports free.

For years these finches did poorly in the East. But in the 1960s and 1970s bird watchers began spotting house finches in growing numbers across state after state. The finches continued to spread westward, living well around farms, cities, and villages on their diet of seeds, fruit, and insects.

They build their nests in buildings, tree cavities, bird boxes, and thick-growing bushes. They usually lay four or five eggs.

The house finch may be confused with another reddish-tinted sparrow-sized bird, the purple finch, and, in the West, Cassin's finch. Check your bird guide carefully to determine which one is coming to your feeder.

Red-bellied Woodpecker
Melanerpes carolinus

This is the woodpecker whose name does not match its belly. True, there is a slightly reddish tinge to its undersides, but much more prominent is the red on the back of the neck in both sexes and the cap of the male.

The red-bellied is a common woodpecker in southeastern states, north into Minnesota, Wisconsin, and New York, and west into Oklahoma. It is seen in both woodlands and in cities where it comes to feeders in winter. It eats a wide variety of foods, both vegetable and animal, and is one of the woodpeckers that stores food for later use, stashing nuts and seeds under loose bark for recovery when needed.

Both male and female work excavating a nest cavity, usually in a dead tree, and they may reuse the cavity. In the South where growing seasons are longer, these woodpeckers may raise more than one brood a year.

Carolina Wren
Thryothorus ludovicianus

This wren is a common year-round resident through much of the East and Southeast. It comes often to bird feeders in winter. Although it makes use of woodpecker holes, natural cavities and other protected spots for its nest, it also nests in open sheds or garages where it constructs a bulky nest of twigs, leaves, grass, mosses, and bark. An open mailbox may attract it in the nesting season. It is difficult to predict where the wren may nest. I once had a pair build a nest in the bow up my upturned canoe and had to delay my planned river trips until the wren chicks were reared. The usual clutch is five or six spotted eggs which are incubated for two weeks.

Even if you do not see the Carolina wren you will probably hear its song because it sings with the volume turned up. The call is often described as *teakettle, teakettle, teakettle,* with the emphasis on the first syllable.

Greater Roadrunner
Geococcyx californianus

The roadrunner, at home among junipers and cactus, is the clown of the desert. It may be seen in the South and Southwest from Arkansas to California and there is a fair chance that, when seen, it will be running, sometimes at fifteen miles an hour.

Speed helps it capture food, and anything slow enough and small enough, from insects to cotton rats, may go to satisfy its hunger. The roadrunner swallows rattlesnakes, rattles and all. Lizards are a delicacy—especially during the nesting season when there are young roadrunners to feed. There is nothing delicate about the habits of this two-foot-long bird. When it catches a lizard, it may whack it senseless on the nearest rock, then continue to beat it until it is tenderized.

The roadrunner nest, perhaps ten feet above the ground, holds a clutch of three to five eggs which are incubated for twenty days.

Northern Bobwhite

Colinus virginianus

There are other quail native to North America—Gamble's, Mountain, California, Scaled, and Montezuma—but none so widely known as the bobwhite. It belongs to the order *Galliformes,* wild cousins of the barnyard chicken. Because, in some areas, it ranks high among game birds, the bobwhite has been closely studied by biologists striving to keep it at maximum population levels. We know its secrets, that it is a seed eater feeding at ground level, that it needs brushy cover for food, shelter, and safety, and that to keep ahead of the toll taken by predators and other factors, it produces large families of a dozen or more chicks in that nest hidden in the brushy fencerow.

Those of us who grew up in the country remember well this dumpy little brown and white vocalist who stood atop a fencepost repeating its name. In those long-ago days the bobwhite was always there. On any summer day, early or late, you heard it calling from the fields and brushy fencerows. It seems that we hear its call less in this age of large farms and giant fields free of those brushy fencerows, and this is unfortunate because the bobwhite's call brightens the summer day.

American Crow

Corvus brachyrhynchos

In spite of their sins, I've always liked crows, black cousins of the ravens, jays, and magpies. I admired their capacity for getting into trouble while staying out of shotgun range. In the hill country where I grew up, the crow was known as a scoundrel. It nested in the woods and was able to cope with the threats that local farmers made against its life. It adapted to changes that settlers brought to the land and prospered around our farms. We had trouble forgiving the crows for what we sometimes viewed as their sins. My father especially disliked them at corn planting time and with some reason; experienced crows can march down a new row and pluck each tender emerging seedling to glean the grain from which it sprouted. Before laws protected them, the crow's food preferences led people to shoot and poison them and bomb them on their roosts. With the passing years, I admired increasingly the crow's ability to adapt to its changing world. Where once the crow was a country bird, it lives today in the cities, walks our front yards, claims tall inner-city buildings for its community roosts, and nests in parks and along boulevards.

The nest is usually built high in a towering tree where the pair raises four to six young and sounds the crow alarm at the approach of people or other enemies.

American crow, among the more intelligent and resourceful birds, has adapted to cities and villages to become a common yard bird.

Red-tailed Hawk

Buteo jamaicensis

Wherever you travel through the United States, into Mexico, or through much of Canada you can find this large hawk cruising its hunting grounds. It sometimes soars, or perches in a tree, keeping watch for any movement of grasshoppers, mice, rats, squirrels, snakes, cottontails, or other prey. You can recognize it by the reddish upper surface of the tail and the dark broad band across the belly.

In early spring, fortunate observers may witness the red-tailed hawk's spectacular display during the courting season. Two of us once watched in amazement as two pairs of red-tails soared on the thermals over a southern Ohio ridge. One pair came together, seemed to link feet, and tumble through the air together. Then the other pair executed a similar maneuver.

But the performance was topped when two of the birds, apparently one from each pair, approached each other, linked claws and, instead of the usual tumbling, began revolving around each other on a horizontal plane. Their wings did not flap and so they lost altitude, but they clung together in a free fall of perhaps three hundred feet into a timbered area, and not until they were almost at ground level did they separate and save themselves from a crash landing. This was far different from the more common tumbling sometimes performed during courtship, and I later asked Ron Austing about this. Ron, a noted scholar of the red-tailed hawk, said that he had witnessed this display only once in his life, and that time in the autumn. He believes that what we saw was not courtship behavior but an aggressive territorial act between competing hawks. Whatever the motivation, the privilege of seeing this unusual display was one of the memorable high points in a lifetime of birding—proof that there can be surprises awaiting the birder even among the best-known birds.

Bald Eagle

Haliaeetus leucocephalus

To see a bald eagle is a memorable event. Because it is a special bird to Americans, I include it here.

Our national bird, in its adult plumage, is a deep chocolate brown, contrasted with a gleaming white head and tail. It was once much more common than it is today. Although still found throughout much of America, it is a rarity in many states. It came into serious trouble when the chemical insecticide DDT was legally used on farms across the country. DDE, a metabolite of DDT, caused the eagles to lay thin-shelled eggs that broke in the nest. In addition, irresponsible gunners shot eagles. But the use of DDT became illegal and strict enforcement of new laws helped the eagles begin gradually rebuilding their numbers. More recently, biologists became concerned because other chemicals reduced the breeding success of eagles, especially around the Great Lakes. Through much of their range the bald eagles still face an uncertain future.

The exception is in Alaska, where eagles are part of the daily scene. People living along coastal Alaska, and tourists visiting there, see these giant birds by the dozens. In the fishing village of Cordova, I once watched half a dozen eagles squabbling over discarded fish beside the restaurant where I ate breakfast. More were perched in the tall pine trees on the hill above town when I went out the door.

Normally the bald eagle mates for life. The nest, in the top of a towering tree, is view property. Here they raise one or two young a year, bringing them fish until they are old enough to leave home.

Watch for the bald eagle around coastal bays and large lakes and streams. If you live, or vacation, in Florida you have a good possibility of seeing eagles frequently. Elsewhere, winter is a good season to add this spectacular bird to your list. They are often seen in winter below the dams along the Mississippi River.

IV

EQUIPMENT FOR BIRD WATCHERS

Binoculars

Serious bird watchers are about as likely to forget their binoculars as they are to leave their shoes at home. Beginners and old-timers alike depend heavily on these optical aids and with good reason. Binoculars enable a person to get a close look at distant birds. A good pair of binoculars can reveal details in the plumage of a warbler in the treetops, the shape of the bill of a wading bird on the far side of the marsh, or the wing bars on a duck in the middle of the lake.

Most of us setting forth to purchase a new pair of binoculars know little about judging their relative quality or determining which pair will best serve the purpose. Field glasses are dif-

ferent from binoculars. The field glass is simply a double telescope. Light goes directly through from image to eye, and images are magnified by a system of convex and concave lenses. The disadvantages include the narrow width of the field viewed and low power magnification, for which this design is suited. For more powerful glasses, 6× and above, the prism design is superior.

Within each barrel of a pair of prism binoculars are set two prisms that direct the light rays back, then redirect them forward again, and this is the reason binoculars can be shorter than telescopes of the same power would be. The prism system permits higher power magnification and

Binoculars give birder a close-up look at birds found on J.N. "Ding" Darling National Wildlife Refuge on Sanibel Island, Florida. *Rex Gary Schmidt, U.S. Fish and Wildlife Service.*

gathering of more light in a compact instrument.

The inside of a pair of quality prism binoculars is a place of hidden mysteries. It houses a collection of glass in various shapes, all expertly ground, coated, and carefully arranged.

The person expecting to use binoculars over a long time should choose the best instrument he can afford, preferably a well-known brand name with a warranty to indicate the manufacturer's faith in his product. Low-cost binoculars frequently do not have the elements as well mounted and secured as do the higher-priced glasses. And binoculars with a prism out of line after some seemingly slight bump become not only useless but also a strain on the human eye. The better-quality binoculars are likely to hold up better. Good ones should last a lifetime for the average person, whereas those inexpensive jobs may have to be repaired or replaced several times over the years.

Price aside, however, the person about to invest in such equipment should understand some basic binocular terminology. Such numbers as 7×35, 8×40, or 10×50 on binoculars are easily understood. The first figure tells the power of magnification. In a pair of 7×35 binoculars the 7× means that that image of the wood thrush is seven times as large as when seen by the naked eye; stated another way, the binoculars bring it seven times closer to the eye. But glasses too powerful are difficult to use, because they magnify not only image sizes but also movement. The more powerful the binoculars, the more difficulty the user may have holding them steady. The most popular binoculars are those magnifying six, seven, or eight times, with 7×35 an all-time favorite for bird watching and most other field sports and activities. Ten-power binoculars are best suited to special work such as the study of waterfowl or use by bird watchers with much experience in field observation. Before investing in binoculars, see if you can hold them steady in viewing position for at least two minutes.

That second number, the one following the ×, tells the diameter in millimeters of the front, or "objective," lens.

Field of view is the width of the scene, usually at 1,000 yards from the binoculars, and it can vary widely depending on your choice of glasses. A field of view measuring 420 feet at 1,000 yards is common for seven- and eight-power binoculars. The more powerful the binoculars, the narrower the field of view is likely to be. A wide field of view makes it easier to locate objects and follow action.

In addition, consider size and weight when comparing binoculars. This can be especially critical if you also carry cameras or other field equipment. For years I moved about in the field with so much photographic equipment hanging around me that much of the time there was not room for my 7×35 binoculars. They stayed in the car or camp. This was overcome when I purchased a pair of eleven-ounce compact Bushnell binoculars, small enough to fit into a coat pocket. Also, by shortening the strap so they would hang only inches beneath my chin, I could carry them and the cameras even on a long day afield. They were a compromise that solved a problem.

Focusing can be accomplished by either of two systems used in the manufacture of binoculars. Some are made to focus the eyepieces individually. Others are equipped for center focus, and these are generally more desirable because they enable fast focusing of both eyepieces at once. Focusing is necessary, depending on the distance from the viewer to the bird or other object being studied.

Consider again the numbers that describe the binoculars. The 7×35 binocular is a seven-power glass with an *objective* lens (the one that admits light) measuring thirty-five millimeters in diameter. Divide the power into the size of the objective lens and you arrive at the *exit pupil,* which determines the amount of light admitted to the eye. The larger the exit pupil, the brighter the picture. The larger exit pupil is especially helpful in poor light in the woods or early and late in the day. The 7×35 binocular admits a highly satisfactory amount of light for most people most of the time. Those using binoculars at night might need binoculars with a larger, heavier objective lens, for example, a 7×50 figuring out to an exit pupil of 7.1mm.

There are two other factors contributing to the binoculars' ability to gather light and transmit it to the eye. One is the lens coating. Good lenses are normally coated thinly with magnesium fluoride to reduce glare and light loss from the internal optical surfaces. On high-quality binoculars, manufacturers normally coat *all* surfaces of *every* lens. You can check this before buying. Look at the reflections you see when you hold the lens at an angle to a fluorescent light, checking both the eyepiece and the objective lens. Coated surfaces will reflect blues and ambers, and white spots seen among these are from uncoated optical surfaces within the binoculars.

Good-quality glasses give better resolution than do low quality lenses. This means better definition of details such as bill shapes, color patterns, tail coverts, and wing bars, which can help in identification. Again, the best guarantee is to rely on known brands and guarantees, avoiding the low-cost "bargain" binoculars. One way of testing this is to attach a sheet of newspaper to the wall and test to see which pair of binoculars permits you to read the small type at the greatest distance.

Distortion sometimes shows up in binoculars. If the degree of magnification varies in different areas of the field being viewed, some of the straight lines may then appear curved as viewed through the binoculars.

If you wear eyeglasses, select binoculars that will be comfortable when used in conjunction with them. Some binoculars come equipped with fold-down or retractable rubber or plastic eyecups on the oculars. These are designed to hold the instrument at the correct distance from the eye or from the eyeglasses.

Still another feature useful on binoculars is a lens cap or rain guard, attached with a cord so it can be flipped off the lens for viewing.

Spotting Scopes

Binoculars may not provide enough magnification for study of distant birds, and because of this some bird watchers also invest in spotting scopes. The most widely chosen is a twenty-power scope, although they are commonly available, usually at sporting-goods or gun stores, at powers ranging from fifteen to sixty. The higher the magnification, the bigger the problems from movement. The twenty-power scope is generally ample for the birder. There are zoom telescopes that offer varying degrees of magnification, ranging, for example, from twenty- to forty-five-power in a single instrument.

The field of view can vary between scopes, and it decreases as power increases. Wide-angle scopes are more satisfactory for viewing larger areas, such as those that might be occupied by rafting ducks, without excessive movement. A

Whatever the spotting scope selected, the birder will need a strong tripod because the scope magnifies motion.

common field of view with a twenty-power scope is 120 feet at 1,000 yards.

Spotting scopes, because they magnify motion, generally require some support other than human hands if they are to be satisfactorily used. I have handled gunstock mounts that enable a bird watcher to steady his spotting scope well enough for most field observation. Lightweight telescoping monopods also help greatly in reducing movement in a spotting scope. One good answer if you watch waterfowl or other birds from your car is a window mount that clamps directly to the glass when the window is rolled down enough to accommodate it. But the best answer is a substantial tripod that will hold the scope steady even in a moderate wind. The same tripod can be used for a camera mount. With proper adapter rings the spotting scope can also be fitted to some cameras, although the optical quality and photographic results may never equal those obtainable with the regular telephoto lens made especially for photography.

Birder on wildlife refuge takes advantage of permanently mounted spotting scope to scan the marsh.

Window mount for spotting scope enables birder to use car as a blind.

Birders and Their Computers

Serious birders, and even some of the more casual ones, are turning to computers to help modernize their record keeping. This was inevitable. When kept in longhand, a birder's records often are skeletal. But once transferred to a disk, they can easily and quickly preserve all manner of interesting details about the bird, habitat, weather, and the trip.

Furthermore, the computer can retrieve this information quickly, as well as dig out the answers to complex questions. Once the records are on a disk, the computer can answer such

```
Sighting File    Reports   Places   Journal   Checkl   Options   Utils   coLors
                  ┌── In checklists of these states, * = seen ──┐i\bird\data
     Crested M    │                     Bell's Vireo            │
VIREOS           │ No East - NH NJ NY                          │
  * White-eye    │ So East - AL FL KY MS NC SC TN              │
    Thick-bil    │ So Cent - AR KS LA OK TX                    │
  * Bell's Vi    │ No Cent - IL IN IA MI MN*MO NE ND OH SD WI  │
    Black-cap    │ Rky Mtn - CO NV UT WY                       │
    Gray Vire    │ So West - AZ NM                             │
  * Solitary     │ Pacific - CA OR                             │
  * Yellow-th    │ WCan+AK -                                   │      r
    Hutton's     │ CentCan - ON                               │
  * Warbling     │ EastCan -                                   │
  * Philadelp    │ Hawaii  -                                   │
  * Red-eyed     │                  In 35 states              │
    Yellow-gr    │ F1 Help  F2 Add  F4 Delete  F8 Show All  Esc Quit │bler
    Black-whi    └────────────────────────────────────────────┘
    Yucatan Vireo                      * Black-throated Gray Warbler
WOOD-WARBLERS                          * Townsend's Warbler
    Bachman's Warbler                    Hermit Warbler
  * Blue-winged Warbler                * Black-throated Green Warbler
  * Golden-winged Warbler                Golden-cheeked Warbler
        975 species in Master Checklist - 237 seen
    (Ctrl)PgUp   (Ctrl)PgDn   ↑ ↓ → ←   Home   End   ←┘ = Select
F1-Help 2-Add 3-Edt 4-Del 5-FxDt 6-FxPl 7-FxCom 8-Where 9-Find 10-Next Esc-Quit
```

Today's birders can select computer software that allows them to update observations and keep detailed records on disks. This is a screen from AviSys Birding Software Systems by Perceptive Systems, P.O. Box 1908, Lafayette, CA 94549.

questions as how many female downy woodpeckers did I see in Indiana in December between July 1, 1984, and July 1, 1992. Or, what raptors did I see in the birdathon in 1989?

The earliest commercially available software program for birders came to the market about 1987, and five years later there were perhaps half a dozen of them being offered. They are mostly written for use on IBM compatibles although there is at least one available for owners of Apple computers. They are generally on a single disk and are priced between $60 and $90. The companies selling software for birders advertise in birding magazines.

Birders who own computers can also tap into networks of birders including members in distant states and countries. Subscribers to one such network, BirdChat, use their modems to flash news of rare and interesting bird sightings across the country as fast as they can come in from their field trips and settle before their computers.

Clothes

Much bird watching admittedly is under rather gentle conditions where clothes may not be a major item of concern. There is, however, always the possibility that the sudden flashing colors of some unknown bird will lure people into heavier cover and have them wishing they had been prepared. Most serious bird watchers have perfected and standardized their field outfit. These clothes need not be much different from the same comfortable but rugged clothing worn by hunters, fishermen, and hikers.

Bird watchers should select their field clothes more for comfort and protection than high style.

Shoes are of particular importance. All bird watchers, contrary to what you may hear, do not wear tennis shoes. My favorite outdoor shoe, summer and winter, is an eight-inch all-leather boot waterproof or treated to be water-repellent. Such shoes should have nonskid soles, enabling one to climb around on rocky surfaces safely. I like the added support that these boots give and the comfort they provide through a full day's wear.

When you are looking for marsh birds, or when the weather is wet, boots with rubber lower parts and leather upper sections are a good choice. These can be purchased from mail-order outdoor stores, such as L.L. Bean, and sometimes from sporting-goods stores. Outdoor shoes should be at least ankle-high to provide protection against rocks, briars, and thorns.

Remember thermal underwear for those chilly days, and insulated underwear for extremely cold weather. Carry a spare pair of socks in pocket or day pack for a midday change if your feet get wet.

Bird watchers who don't get out of sight of their automobiles need have little concern about rain, but most will want to prepare for longer hikes and the possibility of storm or showers. Lightweight plastic raincoats are helpful protection against showers, but heavy brush may tear them. More rugged rainsuits or oilskins offer better protection. A broad-brimmed hat helps to keep rain from running down your neck. A sheet of lightweight plastic under which you can huddle and wait out a storm will be welcome and is especially advisable if you are carrying cameras that need protection. Likewise, a Space Blanket, obtainable at sporting-goods stores, is wet-weather insurance and particularly useful when you are traveling by boat or canoe.

For cool weather a pair of lightweight cotton gloves is handy.

For trips afield on bitter cold days a pocket hand warmer is an added luxury.

The hand warmer, a small first-aid kit, lunch sack, and Thermos bottle can all be carried together in a small day pack that fits over the shoulders and leaves hands free for the use of binoculars, cameras, and notebooks. Day packs with special zippered compartments for various items are available from sporting-goods stores.

If you search for birds in wild areas, a good compass has a place in your equipment. Depending on its design, it may be carried in your pocket, pinned on your coat, or worn on your wrist. The rule when purchasing a compass is to buy a good one, then trust it.

Bird Lists and Notes

Bird watchers normally carry printed check lists that include all the bird species likely to be found in the state or region. There are bird lists available for cities, states, individual nature preserves, national parks, national forests, national wildlife refuges, and other areas. It is frequently possible to obtain such bird lists from park or forest headquarters, sometimes free, sometimes at minimal cost. Bird lists may be obtained from local Audubon societies, bird clubs, nature centers, and natural history museums. Staff members of these organizations usually know if such lists are available and where to get them. A good list is sold by American Birding Association, P.O. Box 6599, Colorado Springs, CO 80934.

In addition to a bird list, the birder may want to carry a pocket notebook, perhaps a small spiral-bound notebook that fits a shirt pocket. If you are the note taking type you may use it for recording details on the flight pattern of a flicker, the song of a catbird, the wing markings of a pine grosbeak, or the nest placement of a mallard, perhaps complete with pencil sketches. All such notes should include date, place, details on weather, and time of day. This brand of field observation adds interest to the hours afield and can result in information of scientific value.

These skeleton field notes, however, may deserve end-of-the-day elaboration in a more permanent record book. This record-keeping can be of interest for years to come, especially if observations are on species undergoing changes in status.

V

ATTRACTING BIRDS

Homes for Birds

Around our homes, farms, parks, gardens, and even the woodlands, the trend is toward tidiness, and weedy fields, bushy fence rows, dead trees, and thick undergrowth give way to manicured countryside. New subdivisions with neat, almost sterile, chemically-treated lawns appear where there were farm fields only a few years earlier. The birds that once occupied these areas often vanish with the changing habitat.

But almost anywhere people live they can still have a variety of birds around their homes because they can take positive steps to entice them. Yards can be planned and planted with thought to the needs of birds, while bird housing and water can help to draw the feathered clan in. It is neither difficult nor particularly costly to have a variety of birds in full view the year around. Bird boxes ready for the nesting season can encourage several native birds to establish family territories where people can watch their behavior.

Birdhouses of many designs can be purchased at garden or hardware stores and nature centers. But for numerous families with basic shop tools at hand, building birdhouses provides an excellent project for long winter evenings. This is a family enterprise that retains its interest well beyond the shopwork phase. Into the summer nesting season, the birdhouses are watched for signs of acceptance by wrens, bluebirds, screech owls, or other species for which they might be intended.

The following list includes some of the numerous bird species that will accept artificial nesting structures.

BIRDS KNOWN TO USE NEST BOXES OR PLATFORMS

Bluebird	Tufted titmouse
White-breasted nuthatch	Robin
Carolina chickadee	House wren
Black-capped chickadee	Bewick's wren
Carolina wren	Downy woodpecker
Tree swallow	Hairy woodpecker
Barn swallow	Screech owl
Cliff swallow	Saw-whet owl
Purple martin	Barn owl
House sparrow	Great horned owl
Bronzed grackle	American kestrel
Starling	Mourning dove
Phoebe	Wood duck
Crested flycatcher	American goldeneye
Yellow-shafted flicker	Hooded merganser
Red-headed woodpecker	

Depending on the kind of bird for which the house is intended, it can be constructed in any of a wide variety of designs and sizes ranging from the elaborate colony structures for purple martins to the simple platforms wired into the crotches of trees for the doves. Doves never learned to build quality housing for themselves. They settle instead for a flimsy platform of sticks loosely arranged on a limb. But by supplying a small shallow basket made of hardware cloth and wired to a crotch in the tree limb, a friend of the doves can often entice them to use this artificial foundation for their homesite and improve their chances of successfully raising their young. Doves have also been known to utilize berry baskets or those little wicker baskets of the kind used for hot rolls. They should be wired securely in place six to twelve feet above the ground.

It is generally a better plan to supply boxes for a variety of bird species than to erect several of the same kind in the same area. Within a species, birds are territorial, and most of them will not tolerate intrusions by others of their kind into their territories. Territories of different species, however, will overlap. A pair of bluebirds that might not nest near other bluebirds may still nest quite close to a pair of chickadees or mourning doves.

Birdhouse Pointers

Wood is the most suitable, all-around building material. Do not use tin cans because summer sun may kill the occupants.

Natural finishes or dull colors are better for exteriors than bright colors, except for martin houses, which should be painted white to reflect the sun.

Do not make the entrance hole too large.

Clean old nest materials out of birdhouses well ahead of the time for migrants to return in spring.

A few small holes in the nest box floor will permit drainage if rain blows in.

Ventilation gives greater comfort, and this can be accomplished with a few small holes or slits through the walls beneath the roof overhang.

Build houses so they can be easily opened for cleaning.

Remember that climbing predators, especially cats, are a threat to nesting birds. Protect the birds with metal posts or metal guards on posts.

Species	Length and width Inches	Depth of cavity Inches	From entrance to floor Inches	Diameter of entrance Inches	Height above ground Feet
Bluebird	5 × 5	8	6	1½	4-6
Chickadee	4 × 4	8-10	6-8	1⅛	4-15
Titmouse	4 × 4	8-10	6-8	1¼	6-15
Nuthatch	4 × 4	8-10	6-8	1⅜	12-20
House wren	4 × 4	6-8	4-6	1-1¼	6-10
Bewick's wren	4 × 4	6-8	4-6	1-1¼	6-10
Carolina wren	4 × 4	6-8	4-6	1½	6-10
Violet-green swallow	5 × 5	6	5	1½	10-15
Tree swallow	5 × 5	6	5	1½	10-15
Purple martin	6 × 6	6	1	2½	15-20
Prothonotary warbler	6 × 6	6	4	1⅛	2-4
Crested flycatcher	6 × 6	8-10	6-8	2	8-20
Flicker	7 × 7	16-18	14-16	2½	6-20
Golden-fronted woodpecker	6 × 6	12-15	9-12	2	12-20
Red-headed woodpecker	6 × 6	12-15	9-12	2	12-20
Downy woodpecker	4 × 4	9-12	6-8	1¼	5-15
Hairy woodpecker	6 × 6	12-15	9-12	1½	12-20
Screech owl	8 × 8	12-15	9-12	3	10-30
Saw-whet owl	6 × 6	10-12	8-10	2½	12-20
Barn owl	10 × 18	15-18	4	6	12-18
Kestrel	8 × 8	12-15	9-12	3	10-30
Wood duck	10 × 18	10-24	12-16	4	10-20

Most birds do not need perches on the front of the box, and perches can aid predators in raiding the bird home.

Inner surfaces of the house should be rough so young birds can better cling to the sides when the time comes to leave home.

Face the entrance away from prevailing winds.

A deep woods is a poor location for most birdhouses, but the edge of the woods may be excellent.

DIMENSIONS FOR OPEN PLATFORMS

Species	Dimensions	Height above ground
Robin	7" × 8"	6-15 feet
Barn swallow	6" × 6"	8-12 feet
Phoebe	6" × 6"	8-12 feet

Bluebirds

That favorite symbol of spring, the bluebird has long been prominent on the rural ago, and in villages and cities as well. These members of the thrush family, noted for their bright blue color and their soft warbling song, were seen over the open fields and around the orchards. On any summer day bluebirds could be seen perched on some post or branch, occasionally dropping down to the grass to capture an insect or perhaps taking their prey on the wing. They were a symbol, correctly or otherwise, of gentleness and love. I have never heard of a person who considered bluebirds an enemy of man.

The nest was always in a cavity. It might have been in a hole chiseled by woodpeckers in the limb of an apple tree. Or it might have been a cavity in a weathered wooden fence post.

But times change. Little farms have been combined to form big farms. Miles of old fences have vanished. For the fences that do remain, the once-common wooden posts have been replaced by steel posts. Meanwhile, orchards are

trimmed more carefully, and hollow limbs are harder for nest-building birds to find.

Most seriously, perhaps the world of the bluebird has been changed by man's introduction and release of foreign bird species. One problem bird is the house sparrow. People who thought they wanted sparrows released them in the early 1800s and to their joy saw the dingy little brownish birds prosper and, in the following years, begin to spread. The feisty sparrows went right on spreading and muscling into the territories of native bird species across the country,

Bluebird houses can be erected at edge of open grasslands where the birds hunt insects. The extra block at the entrance of this house is added predator protection.

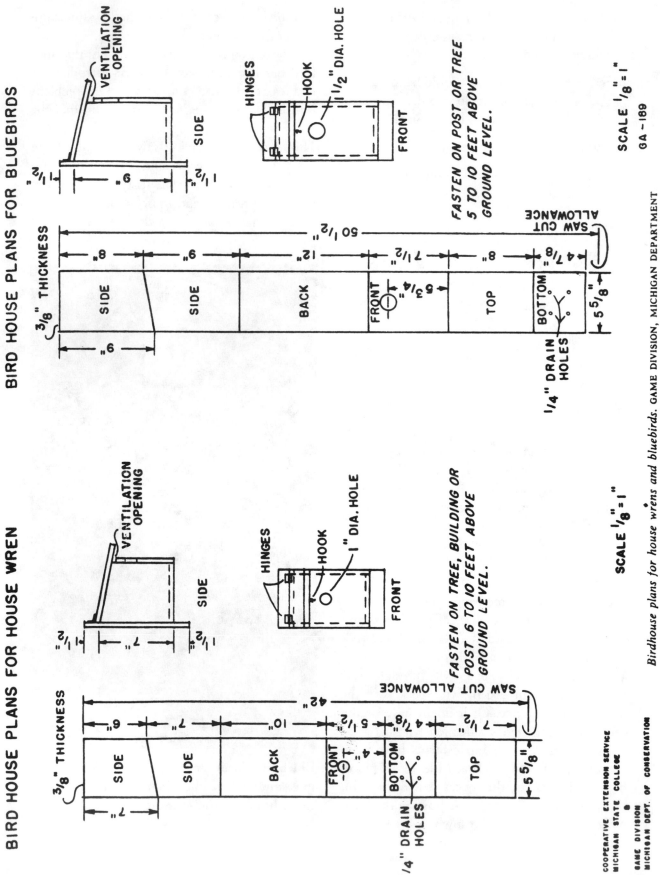

BIRD HOUSE PLANS FOR BLUEBIRDS

BIRD HOUSE PLANS FOR HOUSE WREN

Birdhouse plans for house wrens and bluebirds. GAME DIVISION, MICHIGAN DEPARTMENT OF CONSERVATION AND COOPERATIVE EXTENSION SERVICE, MICHIGAN STATE COLLEGE

fighting and competing continuously for every available nesting space. The bluebirds are noted for arriving early in the spring. But the sparrows have been there all winter. And even on a winter day they may be seen transporting a wide variety of nesting materials into any space they can claim. In addition, they have been known to kill bluebirds outright by invading their nest boxes.

The European starling is an even more serious problem. These antagonistic blackbirds, like the house sparrows that preceded them, prospered and spread. Any effort to rescue the bluebird is automatically a fight against the starling.

Some years ago our region of the country suffered two successive winters with abnormally low temperatures. There were days when the thermometer dropped to 25 degrees below zero, and the cold weather persisted. Birds could neither find sufficient food to supply the energy needed to survive, nor travel far enough to escape the punishing weather. Bobwhites, Carolina wrens, and bluebirds all plummeted, and populations were low for several years. Concern for the bluebirds prompted those who liked to have them around to build and erect more bluebird houses, and this perhaps played a role in the recovery of these favorite birds. One of the bluebird houses we put up in those years went empty the first year or two. Then we heard the bluebird again on a spring day, and a pair found the empty box and moved in. Every year since this box has been home to two or three broods of bluebirds. They seem now to be as common as ever, and I think the new boxes helped them return.

Bluebird nest boxes should be ready for the occupants early in the year, by February 15 in the South and by March 15 in northern states. The female bluebird will produce three to six eggs, usually blue, then incubate them for thirteen or fourteen days without any help from her mate. The young are in the nest from two to three weeks, during which time both parents carry food to them almost continuously during the daylight hours. After they leave the box,

however, the male takes over and provides whatever additional care the young need because the female has already started searching for a nest site for her second brood. Occasionally she will raise three broods in a year. For this reason bluebird nest boxes should be made so they can be easily opened and cleaned out shortly after the brood departs. The female may use the same box for her second nest.

Bluebird boxes should be made of wood, and the box need not be fancy nor the materials costly. What it must have, however, is close attention to the required measurements, especially the entrance, because the size of the entrance is the key to creating a bluebird house that starlings can't get into. The entrance needs to be exactly one and a half inches in diameter. If it is much smaller, the bluebird cannot enter, and if it is much larger, the starling will get into the box. The bottom of this doorway should be at least six inches above the floor to prevent starlings from perching at the hole and destroying eggs and young, or even killing the adult as she sits on the nest. The bottom of the bluebird box should be five inches square.

The finished box, which need not be painted but may be stained, should be set on a post, preferably at the edge of a clearing facing into the clearing with the entrance away from the prevailing winds and rain. Somewhere out in front of the box, to provide a ready refuge for the newly emerging young, should be a tree that can be reached with a flight of perhaps no more than seventy-five feet. If the bottom of the bluebird box is about five feet above the ground, it is satisfactory to the birds and out of reach of some of the predators that might plague them. The box does not need a perch. Added predator protection can be offered by placing a metal cone or metal sleeve around the post below the box, or if galvanized metal posts are used, the metal can be greased during the summer months to keep it too slippery for predators to climb.

Start a Bluebird Trail

From scattered locations comes encouraging news of a resurgence of the bluebird because of human benefactors. Says Lorne Scott of his neighborhood around Indian Head, Saskatchewan, "People report seeing bluebirds for the first time in ten, twenty, or thirty years. And still others tell of seeing their very first bluebird." Bluebirds are returning to that section of Canada almost certainly because of what Scott, and others, now call their "bluebird trails." Some such trails may extend for only two or three miles, others for hundreds of miles.

While still a high school student, Scott began making bluebird houses and erecting them

Building bird houses is a family-style project, fun for young and old alike. These birdhouses began with a section of hollow cherry log. Once the log is prepared, an entrance hole is drilled in one side, floor and roof attached, and house is ready for placing in a tree, on a post, or side of outbuilding.

around his family's farm. Each year he added more houses. His string of bluebird houses stretched down the country road away from the farm, with two to five new bluebird houses going up along each new mile of trail.

Then Scott met John Lane at a meeting of the Saskatchewan Natural History Society, and both learned they were engaged in similar projects. They also discovered that their trails were heading toward each other, and the following year Scott and Lane joined their birdhouse trails. Three years later Scott and the Saskatoon Junior Natural History Society linked trails at Raymore, Saskatchewan, and together these bird watchers now maintained what became known as the longest bluebird trail in the world. In Manitoba and Saskatchewan, there were soon more than two thousand miles of these trails along back country roads and major high-

ways, including the TransCanada Highway. Lane and the Brandon Bird Club erected more than four thousand birdhouses along fourteen hundred miles of bluebird trails, and Scott believes that more than ten thousand bluebird houses were erected in these two provinces by individuals, natural history clubs, Scout troops, and school classes.

This string of houses requires the efforts of many bird watchers each year to clean and maintain the bluebird homes. Most of the houses attract occupants; many of those not occupied by bluebirds provide residences for tree swallows. Ordinarily these houses are made of unpainted plywood and erected in clearings, on fence posts about five feet above the ground. In Manitoba and Saskatchewan, bluebird watchers know that house building can help bring the bluebird back.

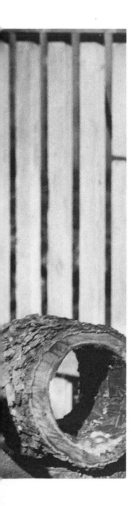

Kestrel Trail

Another kind of nesting box trail, this one for the American kestrel (formerly called sparrow hawk), had its beginning in Iowa in 1983. That year a biologist with the Iowa Department of Natural Resources obtained permission from the state Department of Transportation to attach kestrel nest boxes to the backs of those large information signs erected along interstate highways. The bluejay-sized hawks find good hunting for grasshoppers and small rodents in the median strips and nearby meadows. That first year, twenty nest boxes were erected and eight of them were promptly occupied by kestrels.

Since then, new boxes have been added until the trail of nest boxes stretches across the whole state along I-35 from Minnesota to Missouri. Other states have adopted the plan as volunteers offered to help build and erect the boxes. In Iowa, about half of the boxes are used by kestrels, and seventy percent of those used produce young birds successfully.

The steel posts on which the highway signs are erected render these nest boxes largely predator-proof. The boxes are attached to the posts with metal bands at heights of ten to thirty feet, and higher ones seem to be more attractive to the kestrels. Once in place the boxes require annual maintenance and monitoring.

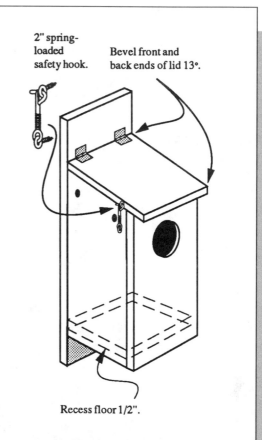

2" spring-loaded safety hook.

Bevel front and back ends of lid 13°.

Recess floor 1/2".

To hold the roof secure and allow for easy cleaning access, hinge the roof and use a spring-loaded safety hook .
Place 3" of wood chips, wood shavings, or straw in bottom of box.

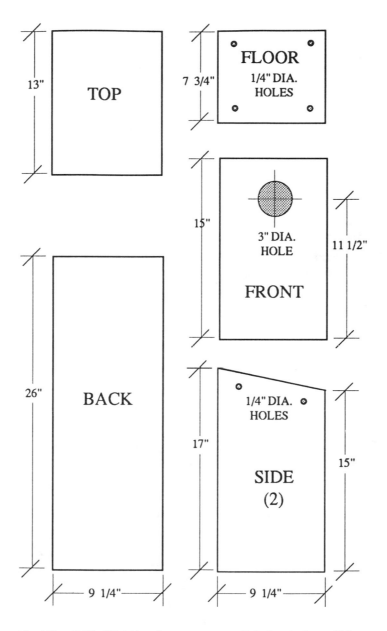

13" TOP

7 3/4" FLOOR
1/4" DIA.
HOLES

15"   3" DIA.
        HOLE
        FRONT   11 1/2"

26" BACK

1/4" DIA.
HOLES

17"   SIDE
        (2)   15"

9 1/4"   9 1/4"

LUMBER: One 1" x 10" x 8' 0", (#2 white pine recommend). Painting the box will increase its useful life.
HARDWARE: Twenty-two 1 1/2" wood screws (#6), two 2" hinges and one 2" spring-loaded safety hook.

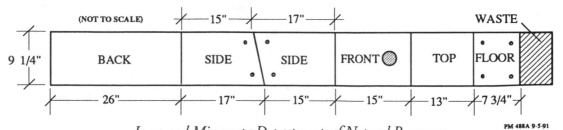

(NOT TO SCALE)   15"   17"   WASTE

9 1/4" BACK   SIDE   SIDE   FRONT   TOP   FLOOR

26"   17"   15"   15"   13"   7 3/4"

Iowa and Minnesota Departments of Natural Resources.

PM 488A 9-5-91

Purple Martins and People

The purple martin, largest of the swallows, noted for its dark color, forked tail, long wings, and skillful aerial maneuvering throughout the daylight hours, is a long-time favorite. Even before white men found this continent, earlier people were putting up homes for the martins. Some Indians commonly made martin colonies by hanging gourds in saplings outside their doorways. This is the bird of which Alexander Sprunt, Jr., once said, "Young and old admire it, encourage it, and protect it, and those who have a word of criticism for it are few and far between." Farmers frequently encourage the martins by erecting martin houses around their stockyards, and fruit growers find that they are an aid in controlling fruit flies. Others like purple martins simply because they enjoy watching them fly, hearing their calls, and knowing that the lower insect population adds to the pleasures of porch sitting on a summer evening.

Under natural conditions purple martins nested in hollow trees, often using abandoned woodpecker holes. But today's purple martins have been quick to take up residence in man-made martin houses. A number of communities across the country have declared the purple

Commercially made martin houses are available from garden and birding-supply stores. This twelve-room apartment house is equipped with telescoping pole for easy cleaning. *Nature House, Inc.*

Because martins are colonial nesters they require large, complex houses. Once they move in, they usually return year after year. Meanwhile, the house must be cleaned and made ready for them.

martin their favorite wild citizen and have organized community-wide programs to attract them. Most famous of all such "martin towns" is Griggsville, Illinois. Tourists travel to Griggsville just to see the purple martins and the dozens of big birdhouses lining the main street. To promote the welfare of the purple martin, citizens have organized into the Griggsville Wild Bird Society, a purple martin fan club devoted to aiding what is known in that part of Illinois, as "man's best summer friend."

Nobody knows how many purple martins live in and around Griggsville, but one thing is certain: There are far more of them now than there were in 1962. That year the town fathers decided to do something about the insects that plagued them. J. L. Wade, a manufacturer of television antennas, had an idea: Instead of investing funds in a chemical insecticide and risking ecological threats, why not invite the purple martins to town? Wade went one step further and had engineers in his company design an aluminum purple martin house with a telescoping pole. This became the prototype

What is probably the world's largest purple martin housing complex stands in Griggsville, Illinois.

for standard martin apartment houses around Griggsville, and it proved so popular elsewhere that Wade subsequently added martin houses to his line of commercial products. Twenty-eight of these new houses were soon erected on metal poles around Griggsville, and, according to the town fathers, the results were immediately evident, with a surprising 80 per cent of the spaces in the new birdhouses occupied that first year. According to Wade, citizens who had older martin houses complained that their long-time resident martins were leaving them and moving into the new housing.

The birds patrolled Griggsville's skies, consuming uncounted numbers of mosquitoes, flies, and other insects. Townspeople claimed that, for the first time in years, they could enjoy backyard cookouts.

So successful was this plan that the Griggsville Jaycees enlarged the program the following year, and their town soon had more apartment houses for birds than it did for people. At the fairgrounds, where insects were always a major problem around the livestock barns, the jubilant fair manager no longer had to follow his longtime practice of purchasing chemical insecticides.

Gradually word of Griggsville's success with the purple martin spread to other parts of the country. Lake Charles, Louisiana; Fort Smith, Arkansas; Bass Lake, Indiana; Lenox, South Dakota; Trenton, New Jersey; and Cleveland, Ohio, were among the cities that launched martin housing programs. Martins seem to like living near people. Citizens carrying out their normal activities around the yard do not disturb the birds. And no matter how many martins invade a community, their human neighbors seem never to tire of them.

The worst enemies of the purple martin are house sparrows and starlings. But the builders of modern martin houses found ways to defeat them and keep the bird apartments vacant for martins. Houses must be erected so they can be easily lowered for cleaning out old nests and the debris air-freighted in by intruders.

The telescoping metal pole can be lowered while martins are in residence without endangering nest, eggs, or young.

Once the martins have departed for the year, entrances to the rooms are capped shut until the following spring.

Martin houses should be placed in the open where there are no close obstructions such as trees or buildings. An elevation of fifteen or twenty feet above ground is satisfactory to the birds. How many rooms a martin house will have is determined largely by the ambition of the person who builds it. Houses with nine rooms are common for a start. Rarely is there a martin house as large as the record-size structure that tourists photograph in the center of Griggsville. This housing complex had 504 compartments.

Each room should measure six inches square. The entrance should have a diameter of two inches, and the bottom of the entrance should be one and a half inches above the floor. A deck in front of the entrance gives the birds a place to perch and the young a launching platform on that eventful day when they are ready to take wing.

Some bird watchers like their martin houses to express the builder's personality. Large, small, fancy, plain, it is all the same to the birds, provided they are given protection from sparrows and starlings, and their houses are clean and waiting in spring when martins return from their Amazon Basin wintering grounds.

Invite the Wood Ducks

Another bird willing to use artificial nesting boxes is the wood duck, ordinarily considered America's most beautiful waterfowl. Those fortunate enough to have marshes, ponds, or woodland streams on or near their property within the breeding range of this duck may be able to attract the mated pairs.

Under natural conditions, this cavity-dwelling duck rears its brood in a hollow tree. As civilization advanced, the number of nesting cavities

Baby wood duck gets a first look at the outside world as it prepares to leap from its home to the water below. *Don Cook.*

Pair of wood ducks at nest box, male on box, female at entrance. Note the predator guard. *Don Cook.*

WOOD NEST BOX
FOR WOOD DUCKS

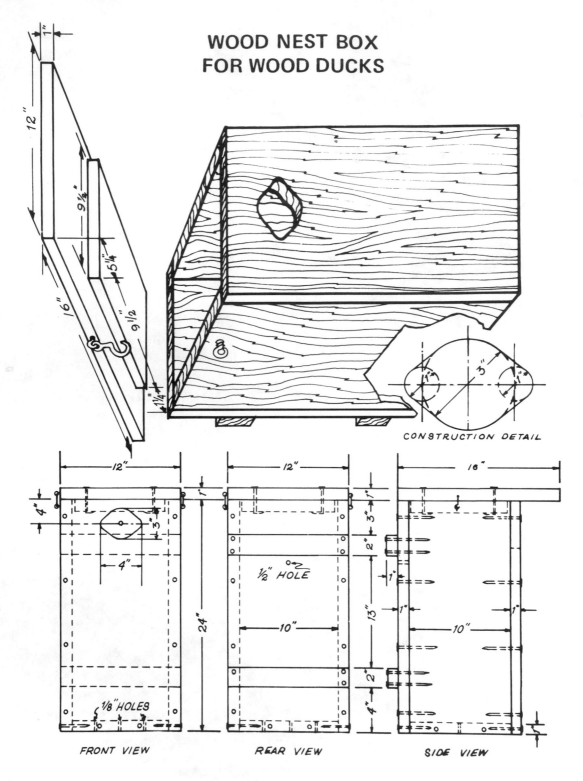

CONSTRUCTION DETAIL

FRONT VIEW   REAR VIEW   SIDE VIEW

ILLINOIS NATURAL HISTORY SURVEY

METAL NEST BOX
FOR WOOD DUCKS

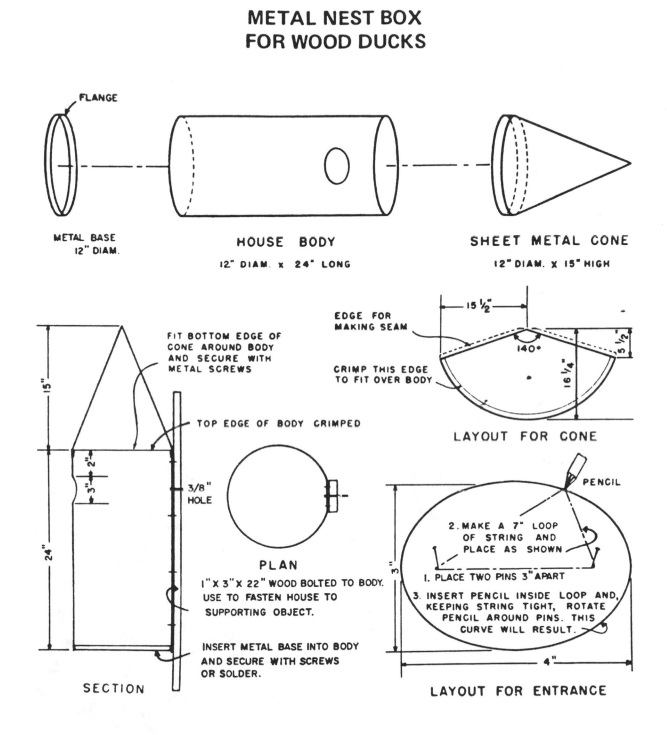

FLANGE

METAL BASE
12" DIAM.

HOUSE   BODY

12" DIAM. x 24" LONG

SHEET METAL CONE

12" DIAM. x 15" HIGH

15"

FIT BOTTOM EDGE OF
CONE AROUND BODY
AND SECURE WITH
METAL SCREWS

EDGE FOR
MAKING SEAM

15 ½"

140°

5 ½"

16 ¼"

CRIMP THIS EDGE
TO FIT OVER BODY

LAYOUT FOR CONE

TOP EDGE OF BODY CRIMPED

2"

3"

3/8"
HOLE

24"

PENCIL

2. MAKE A 7" LOOP
OF STRING AND
PLACE AS SHOWN

3"

1. PLACE TWO PINS 3" APART

3. INSERT PENCIL INSIDE LOOP AND,
KEEPING STRING TIGHT, ROTATE
PENCIL AROUND PINS. THIS
CURVE WILL RESULT.

4"

PLAN

1" X 3" X 22" WOOD BOLTED TO BODY.
USE TO FASTEN HOUSE TO
SUPPORTING OBJECT.

INSERT METAL BASE INTO BODY
AND SECURE WITH SCREWS
OR SOLDER.

SECTION

LAYOUT FOR ENTRANCE

ILLINOIS NATURAL HISTORY SURVEY

available to them diminished, and meanwhile, the birds were taken heavily by overshooting until the season was finally closed completely on them in 1918. Because sportsmen and others found they could encourage wood ducks to use artificial nest boxes, these remarkable birds have recovered from their hazardously low population levels.

Wood-duck nest boxes have been constructed of either wood or metal. Old packing boxes and nail kegs have been put into service for the purpose. One Tennessee conservationist found that wood ducks will occupy duplex houses. He then found a supply of empty shell boxes and turned these ammunition containers into two-family apartments by building a partition in the center, providing each half with an entrance, and erecting the houses in wood-duck country.

Another widely occupied wood-duck box design came out of Illinois some years ago. It is a cylindrical structure formed of twenty-six-gauge metal into a compartment twenty-four inches long with a twelve-inch diameter. The roof is cone shaped, fifteen inches high, and secured by metal screws.

Wooden boxes should be constructed of cypress, if available, or fir, and left unfinished, because the rough inner surfaces enable young ducks to climb out to join their mother on the pond below when she calls them into the outside world. A strip of hardware cloth nailed to the inside of the box, below the entrance, also helps the young birds to climb to the doorway.

Nest boxes should be erected either over water or close to it at heights of ten to twenty-five feet above water level. Predators are a major threat to the female and her eggs and young.

This horizontal nesting structure made from two cylinders of 1"x 2" welded wire, sandwiching a layer of coarse grass, attracts mallards and other ducks when erected on a post sunk in the marsh.

Snakes, squirrels, opossums, and raccoons will enter the boxes and destroy the eggs or young when possible. Consequently, those who have studied the wood duck have worked out ways to short-stop predators. It helps to place the wood-duck box on posts in the water with the entrance facing away from shore. In such cases the boxes can be as low as five feet above high water level. A metal predator guard around the post will keep off raccoons and, if it is tight enough, snakes as well. Some builders of wood-duck boxes have tried suspending them on wires strung between trees, only to find that a raccoon, talented as a tightrope walker, still made its way to the clutch of duck eggs.

If successful, the wood-duck family story goes something like this. On the three inches of clean wood shavings you have placed in the bottom of the box, the female lays one egg each morning until her clutch of ten or twelve is complete. As she lays the seventh egg, she begins to pull some down from her breast to form a soft cover for her eggs. Each day she will add more down, and she will begin incubating on the day after she lays the last egg. The ducklings hatch in about thirty days, and the following morning the female appears at the entrance to her nest box to survey her world. Satisfied that there are no enemies in view, she drops quietly into the water below and begins calling to her ducklings. One by one, they climb the wall to the entrance and with scarcely a pause, leap off. The fortunate bird watcher present at this moment views an unforgettable natural event as the little ducklings heed their mother's call and launch themselves into the outdoor world for the first time. Soon the duck assembles them and guides them to the protection of nearby vegetation. Witnessing this event is a special reward for the work involved in building the nest box. One North Carolina landowner with an eight-acre pond erected five wood-duck boxes which produced 77 ducklings, and the next year, with eight boxes, he saw production rise to 126 on his property. This is a housing project that gets results.

Nest Materials

Birds in the process of nest building will often use nesting materials supplied to them for the purpose. Orioles have been observed pulling lengths of yarn from sweaters hanging on the line and carrying these colorful materials off to their treetop building sites. Acceptable nesting materials include cotton, short strips of cloth, and short pieces of yarn and string. But supply only *short* lengths. Otherwise, the birds may become entangled and be unable to escape. Offer these materials in a special hardware cloth holder, suspended from the low limb of a tree in the vicinity of the nest box. The wire holder in which you offered suet during the winter can double as a container for nesting materials in spring. It should be located where birds can see it easily. Avoid plastic materials. Do not place nesting materials inside a bird box, because birds require an empty space and the opportunity to build their own nests. The exception is found with the cavity-nesting birds such as chickadees, titmice, and woodpeckers. For such species place a layer of sawdust or wood chips two or three inches deep in the bottom of the birdhouse.

❶

❷

❸

❹

❺

1. Blue jay,
   Cyanocitta cristata

2. Carolina chickadee,
   Parus carolinensis

3. Red-winged blackbird,
   Agelaius phoeniceus

4. American redstart,
   Setophaga ruticilla

5. Cape May warbler,
   Dendroica tigrina

6. Bells vireo,
   Vireo bellii

7. Dickcissel,
   Spiza americana

8. Cedar waxwing,
   Bombycilla cedrorum

❻

❼

❽

11

9. Mallard,
    Anas platyrhynchos

10. Canada goose,
    Branta canadensis

11. Bobolink,
    Dolichonyx oryzivorus

12. Rufous-sided towhee,
    Pipilo erythrophthalmus

13. Snowy egret,
    Egretta thula

14. Roseate spoonbill,
    Ajaia ajaia

15. Dark-eyed junco,
    Junco hyemalis

16. Song sparrow,
    Melospiza melodia

17. Greater prairie chicken,
    Tympanuchus cupido

17

12

14

15

16

19

18

20

21

22

18. Tufted titmouse,
    Parus bicolor

19. American robin,
    Turdus migratorius

20. Eastern bluebird,
    Sialia sialis

21. Northern mockingbird,
    Mimus polyglottos

22. Common cardinal,
    Cardinalis, cardinalis

23. Common flicker,
    Colaptes auratus

24. House wren,
    Troglodytes aedon

25. Mourning dove,
    Zenaida macroura

23

25

26

Photo Credits

Karl Maslowski: 1, 2, 3, 8,
12, 15, 16, 18, 19, 20, 21,
22, 23, 24, 25, 29, 32

U.S. Fish and Wildlife
Service/Maslowski: 4, 5,
6, 7, 11, 27

All others by author

29

30

31

28

26. **Evening grosbeak,**
    Coccothraustes vespertinus

27. **Prairie warbler,**
    Dendroica, discolor

28. **American goldfinch,**
    Carduelis tristis

29. **Eastern meadowlark,**
    Sturnella magna

30. **Baltimore oriole,**
    Icterus galbula

31. **Horned puffin,**
    Fratercula corniculata

32. **Yellow warbler,**
    Dendroica petechia

33. **Yellow-headed blackbird,**
    *Xanthocephalus
    xanthocephalus*

33

Brushpiles for Birds

Excellent bird shelter can be quickly provided by making an artificial brush pile in a corner of the garden or lawn. One Connecticut bird watcher recommends that such a shelter be started by leaning large branches loosely against a stump or rock pile. This framework can then be covered with smaller branches and large weeds all arranged loosely. If seed-bearing weeds are included, all the better, because birds using the shelter may feast on them. Following the holiday season, pile the Christmas tree branches on the shelter. If you begin the brush pile with the larger pieces on the bottom, you allow more hiding space in the center of the shelter.

A brush pile is an exceptionally good idea for winter birds that need protection. In a few years, it will settle and decay and a new one may be needed. Vines and bushes planted around can make it more attractive, both to the birds and to the bird watchers who might object to an untidy-looking brush pile in the yard.

Planting for Birds

When you set out to create a "mini-refuge" for the birds, remember that the key word is "variety." Open lawns are important to people and birds alike, but extensive lawns can be broken up by planting vines, shrubs, trees, and flowers, with an eye to both good landscaping and wildlife needs. This can help to compensate for the massive losses of wildlife habitat from our building projects, clearing, drainage, and construction.

The health and survival of birds depend upon the quality of their environment. They must have water and food. And they need shelter to protect them from weather and predators and to provide them with suitable places to nest and roost. The greater the variety of food-producing plants in an area, the better the possibility of seeing a wide variety of birds and other wildlife. People who take their wildlife watching seriously have learned that much can be done to make even a small yard more attractive to birds.

Converting your yard into a bird refuge can begin in any season, but most plantings should

Mourning doves, common around homes and gardens, build their nests in shrubs and trees and, in winter, are attracted to feeding stations if millet and other small seeds are fed at ground level.

be made in spring and fall. Other seasons can be taken up with planning or getting the ground ready for planting. *National Wildlife Magazine* has pointed out that neighbors can combine forces and turn adjoining properties into larger wildlife refuges with a tremendous total impact on wildlife. The magazine suggests that neighbors get together for planning "wildlife neighborhoods" and sharing the costs of plants and seeds. Property values are said to increase by 3 to 10 percent when good vegetation and tree cover are added to the grounds. But more than that, such wildlife-producing properties become living classrooms in ecology, the scene of a never-ending natural show for people privileged to have rabbits, squirrels, hawks, owls, songbirds, and other wild creatures around their homes. Apartment dwellers who may not have any yard to manage can still plant a window box and put out bird feeders and even a small birdbath.

Nursery owners can help in the selection of locally adapted plants particularly good for producing seeds and fruits of value to wildlife. It may not be necessary to purchase expensive shrubs and trees for this purpose. In this age of fast-moving construction projects and endless land clearing, bulldozers cut and bury uncounted thousands of perfectly good wildlife food plants daily. One bird-watching friend of mine is always alert for such building projects. When he finds suitable wildlife plants in the path of the bulldozer, he asks permission of the property owner to dig up the plants and move them. Such plants have a built-in biological advantage, for they are adapted by nature to local conditions. Pin oak, sumac, dogwood, wild cherry, and mulberry are a few of the particularly valuable wildlife food-producing plants sometimes obtainable in this manner.

Another source of plants may be your state conservation department. Some states have regular annual programs for making a variety of plants available at low cost for wildlife plantings.

For something different in plantings, consider creating a miniature "bog" in your backyard. Wetlands are natural areas for a wide variety of beautiful plants and will help to attract a wider variety of birds. One Alabama gardener found she could create a bog area quite easily. She first dug a hole eighteen inches deep. Then she dug out toward the edge of the area, tapering the depth to about eight inches. The deepest part became the wettest portion of the "bog," and here the plants requiring the most moisture established themselves.

A bog area will appear more natural if it is irregular in shape and fits odd corners of the yard or garden. Once the hole is ready, cover the bottom with a layer of heavy-gauge plastic. Next, haul in humus to fill in the hole. Shape this to taper toward the low part of the area as a natural bog would do. In many parts of the country, rainfall will provide water enough to keep the "bog" producing, but water can be sprinkled on it as the need arises. One gardener was so pleased with an artificial bog that she built six more and planted them to a wide variety of ferns and colorful flowers.

Even dead trees have their appeal to birds. In the woods behind my home, dead trees, unless they constitute a hazard, are left to be felled by nature, and once lying on the forest floor they are left where they fall. As they decay, they provide shelter for a wide variety of insects and other invertebrates, which in turn attract birds. These are woodpecker feeding stations. Some years ago a powerful storm broke the tops of four large trees in the woods behind our home. We cleaned up as much as we had to, but left the tree trunks standing for the birds. These dead and slowly decaying trees are searched daily by hungry birds. We see them regularly— brown creepers, nuthatches, and a long list of woodpeckers including the downy, hairy, pileated, red-bellied, and flicker.

Wade H. Hamor, midwestern biologist for the U.S. Soil Conservation Service, has worked out a number of suggestions for making larger acreages on farms, ranches, and other areas into bird refuges. One recommendation is to establish hedgerows especially for birds and other wildlife. The hedgerow can eventually become a six-foot-wide strip of food and cover plants with particular appeal to songbirds. Perhaps the simplest method of establishing a hedgerow is to plow it in late summer or early autumn. Then erect fence posts down the middle of the strip at twenty-foot intervals. To these attach wires on which birds may perch. "Fruit-eating birds," says Hamor, "will plant their choice foods, including wild cherries, blackberries, dogwood, elder, mulberries—and many others." Such natural "plowperch" plantings are said to grow almost as fast as hedgerows that you might establish by setting out the plants yourself.

In addition, a small field can be managed especially for the seed-eating birds by subdividing it into five strips. Plow one of the strips each year and allow it to revegetate naturally. By replowing each strip every fifth year, you keep the field free of large plants and produce a wide variety of vegetation in various stages of maturity. Early invaders into one of these newly plowed strips may include panic grasses, lamb's-quarters, ragweed, smartweed, bristle grass, and other seed-producing species. These will give way in succeeding years to other plants in the ecological succession.

Meanwhile, you may want to plant special food patches for the seed eaters. These food patches can measure anywhere from ten feet square to perhaps a half acre in size. Common crops for these areas are grain sorghum, millet, sunflowers, and corn. Use several kinds of seed to obtain variety.

Do not overlook stream banks and roadsides. Many kinds of birds nest in the grasses and lowgrowing shrubs bordering such areas, and spraying, mowing, burning, and grazing destroy their habitat.

Planting multiflora rose is a bad idea. Although this plant was once actively promoted by government agencies, it quickly became a scourge, as many exotics tend to do. It spreads with the help of birds and takes over whole fields unless the land owner wages a constant battle against it. Some states have passed laws forbidding the planting of multiflora rose.

A pond can become the heart of a wildlife area, but the pond may fail when built by people who lack experience. Start by consulting the office of the U.S. Soil Conservation Service in the nearest county-seat town. This government agency has been responsible for supervising the construction and location of more than 2 million farm ponds across the country. On land with a high water table, ponds can sometimes be constructed simply by digging out small areas.

Marshes can be even more productive than ponds for wildlife. Where there is fairly flat land, tight soil, and a water supply, some birders have succeeded in creating artificial marshes. This kind of project usually calls for construction of a dam or dike. It will not be a deep water area and, for the benefit of wildlife, should not be. Water depth in the finished marsh may range from an inch or two to two or three feet. The marsh may be created in conjunction with a farm pond so that together the area provides water for livestock, fishing, swimming, and wildlife. Artificial marshes generally should have pits dug into them in advance of flooding to provide deeper pothole areas. Wetland vegetation will soon invade such areas naturally, but plantings of shrubs and trees can speed the process and improve the variety.

The following list includes plants that appeal both to birds and to property owners in various regions of the country. Check with local authorities and nurserymen to determine varieties adapted to your area.

VINES THAT ATTRACT BIRDS

Bearberry	Bittersweet
Porcelain vine	Matrimony vine
Virginia creeper	Riverbank grape
Boston ivy	Trumpet honeysuckle
Trumpet	

TEN PLANTS FOR HUMMINGBIRDS

Chinaberry	Morning-glory
Columbine	Nasturtium
Evening primrose	Phlox
Coral bells	Rhododendron
Jewel weed	

PLANTS NEAR POND OR POOL

Buttonbush	Tupelo
Spicebush	Winterberry
Arrowwood	Smooth alder
Hornbean	Juneberry
Larch	Wisteria
Red chokeberry	

FOOD PLANTS FOR WATERFOWL

Sago pondweed	Burr reed
Japanese millet	Duckwheat
Wild rice	Three-square rush
Wild celery	Bulrush
Wapato duck potato	Smartweed
Coontail	Widgeon grass
Reed canary grass	

NORTHEAST AND MIDWEST

Birch, crab apple, dogwood, hawthorn, hemlock, mountain ash, mulberry, red cedar, sassafras, sour gum, spruce, arrowwood, bayberry, black haw, blueberry, blackberry, elderberry, nannyberry, raspberry, snowberry, winterberry, ground juniper, Virginia creeper

SOUTHEAST

Dogwood, mulberry, persimmon, red cedar, sassafras, spruce, American holly, bayberry, blackhaw, blueberry, blackberry, elderberry, raspberry, inkberry, spicebush, winterberry, greenbrier, Virginia creeper

SOUTHWEST

Dogwood, mulberry, persimmon, red cedar, sassafras, sour gum, American holly, black haw, blueberry, elderberry, snowberry, spicebush, greenbrier

ROCKY MOUNTAINS AND GREAT PLAINS

Dogwood, hawthorn, mountain ash, red cedar, spruce, arrowwood, black haw, blueberry, elderberry, nannyberry, snowberry, greenbrier, Virginia creeper

WEST COAST

Crab apple, dogwood, hemlock, mountain ash, red cedar, spruce, blueberry, blackberry, elderberry, snowberry, raspberry, Virginia creeper

Bird Feeders

The best way to bring good numbers of wintering birds close to your window is to offer them food. Nobody knows how many people across the country feed birds or how many tons of grains and other avian edibles are placed before the birds in any calendar year. But on any suburban street a high percentage of residents maintain bird feeders at least during the winter months. Some continue to feed the birds in summer as well.

This may do people as much good as it does the birds. The unending bird show outside the window adds color and interest to the dull winter months. No matter how many times a junco or red-bellied woodpecker visits the bird feeder, each new visit is a treat to those who watch.

When deep snows hide their natural foods, winter birds, such as this song sparrow, still live well as long as the winter feeder supplies their needed energy.

Nearly everyone in any community, can bring at least some birds closer by putting food out for them, and even if they must settle for pigeons, sparrows, and starlings, their life can be richer for the effort. Some bird watchers maintain numerous feeding stations offering all manner of foods to draw the widest possible variety of birds.

A major reward for maintaining a bird feeder is the opportunity it can bring for close-up observation of birds you may previously have seen only from a distance. Chickadees, titmice, downy woodpeckers, nuthatches, cardinals, juncos, and others come to eat outside the window only a few feet from their human observers. Birds become conditioned to this proximity. They gradually learn that there is no danger to them in coming to the feeder. Stay back from the window until birds are coming to the feed regularly, then remember to make no sudden movements that might frighten the sharp-eyed visitors.

A feeder can be moved gradually closer to the window if it is rigged on a pulley and suspended from a wire between the house and a nearby tree or garage. This feeder can also be refilled from the window.

Feeders are often erected on a post five feet or so above ground level. In open areas, feeders may be equipped with wind vane fins so that the wind turns them away from storms.

Feeders can also be suspended from tree limbs or the overhang of a roof, but some birds will not use a free-swinging feeding platform.

The kind of feeder may depend in part on the kinds of feed to be offered on it. Wild birds are commonly fed sunflower seeds, millet, milo, cracked corn, peanuts, wheat, oats, raisins, suet, cut apples, cracked walnuts and hickory nuts, scratch feed, and bread crumbs. Peanut butter is best fed as part of a mixture. Try mixing equal parts of fat and peanut butter; then add six parts of cornmeal. Nuts, raisins, and grain can also be added to this offering.

Juncos and sparrows of many kinds, goldfinches, bobwhites, and some others prefer to eat at ground level. For these ground feeders spread millet, sunflower seed, cracked corn, and scratch feed in a spot that is protected from the weather but separated from heavy cover by an open area so that feeding birds will have warning if predators approach.

Some bird foods, including sunflower seed, have become expensive. The smaller the quantities purchased, the more costly the bird seed is likely to be. Many people who feed birds regularly and use impressive amounts of feed in the course of a winter buy sunflower seed fifty to a hundred pounds at a time. They learn the location of the nearest feed stores and benefit from the lower per-pound prices of quantity purchases.

Buying in quantity can create a storage problem. Kept outdoors or on the porch, the seed may be damaged by weather or broken into by squirrels. Indoors it may attract mice and insects. A few years ago I purchased a plastic trash can with a tight lid capable of holding fifty pounds of sunflower seed. Our resident squirrels promptly chewed through the plastic, ruined the container, and feasted at will on the contents. I replaced this container with a galvanized metal can, which served well until two squirrels, working together, pried the lid from it. By tightening the lid and placing a weight on it, I eventually won out over the squirrels.

A winter supply of suet is especially attractive to such birds as woodpeckers, nuthatches, wrens, brown creepers, titmice, and chickadees. Years ago the butcher would wrap up a couple of pounds of suet without adding anything to the weekly meat bill. But times have changed. Suet has a price today, but for bringing a variety of birds close to the window, it is well worth the cost.

Shops sometimes stock mesh bags that can be filled with beef fat and located where the birds can cling to the netting. Suet can also be offered in wire mesh feeders attached to tree trunks. Suet feeders can be made of rat traps, which keep a grip on the suet as the supply dwindles. If the

This gray squirrel, photographed at an Ohio bird feeder, is especially fond of sunflower seeds and will take over the feeder unless some way can be found to exclude it.

A cloth bag of thistle seed may be nearly hidden by the goldfinches that flock to it in winter.

This kind of feeder, with a storage compartment in the center for mixed seeds, is especially attractive to such birds as cardinals and finches. Squirrels, however, can climb the metal pole unless it is greased or equiped with a metal squirrel guard.

The beehive feeder holds two quarts of sunflower seed and attracts titmice, chickadees, and goldfinches.

Hummingbird feeding on sweetened water. *John Oney.*

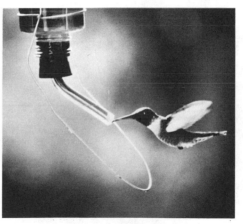

This bent pole with its suspended feeder is an effort to frustrate squirrels and save the seeds for the birds. Squirrels, however, can easily jump from the pole to the top of the feeder.

To make an excellent winter bird feed, add mixed grain to melted suet in which a wire hook is embedded.

Two plastic plates, a piece of wood and a few roofing nails are all the materials needed for this backyard bird feeder.

Even young children can make an effective feeder from a milk carton filled with mixed birdseed.

Revolving feeder made from utility cable spool covered with 2"x4" welded wire fencing can be filled with ear corn. In addition to deer and squirrels, this one attracts crows, jays, cardinals, grouse, and wild turkeys.

A birder knocked the bottom from an old 10-gallon milk can, then set it on small blocks so the 50 pounds of cracked corn, or other grain that it holds, flows out automatically as needed. Feeder serves deer as well as birds.

tongues of birds touch the wire in extremely cold weather, however, they may freeze to the wire surface. One answer is to use rubber-coated wire mesh. Suet can also be placed on the open feeder, but birds carry off large chunks of it, frequently dropping it on the ground.

Another favorite method of offering suet is to melt it in a double boiler, mix in raisins and a variety of seeds, and let it harden into feed cakes, which may be molded into any shape the bird watcher desires. Half a coconut shell makes a good container for such a mixture when suspended where the titmice and chickadees can find it. So does a section of log with one-inch-diameter holes drilled into it. The feeder log is suspended by a hook in one end, and chickadees, wrens, titmice, woodpeckers, and others cling to it and eat the good things offered.

As winter wears on, a bird-feeding station takes on added importance to the birds that have frequented it during the cold months. They have become dependent on its reliable abundance. The feeding center has probably drawn in an abnormally large population of birds, and the late winter weeks are the most hazardous of the year for wildlife. So it is extremely important for the person maintaining a bird feeder not to grow tired of the responsibility and stop feeding the birds. Winter bird feeding, once begun, should be viewed as a responsibility as surely as the care of a pet might be. While on winter vacations, arrange with someone to maintain your feeding station. Keep up the feeding right into spring, when the winter visitors have started to depart for the North again and the breeding season is forcing the permanent residents to spread out into nesting territories.

Chaff and seeds from feeders can be a problem after considerable quantities of it fall to the ground, where chipmunks and mice burrow near these sources of abundant food. Their tunnels can carry water into basements. One

Three methods of feeding beef suit—a choice, high-energy winter bird food—are shown here. Net bag of suet hanging in tree is visited by starling. Wire mesh suet box (opposite, top) attached to tree trunk with wire (not nailed) is popular with woodpeckers such as this red-bellied woodpecker, as well as nuthatches, wrens, chickadees, and others. Rat trap equipped with wire-mesh suet holder (opposite, bottom) prevents waste by keeping pressure on the suet and holding it in place.

The sunflower is highly important to American birds. Its seeds feed millions through the winter months.

answer is to rig a catch tray beneath the feeder, suspending it with small chains. The tray can occasionally be emptied, preferably into the compost heap, where these biodegradable materials are reduced to humus.

In many parts of the country, squirrels are all that stand between the bird watcher and continued sanity. Squirrels learn quickly about new sources of food. Sunflower seeds and other delicacies normally spread on the bird feeder are candy to them. One answer is to relax and become a squirrel watcher. These nimble-footed aerialists are entertaining creatures, and I would surely not like to have them all vanish from the little woodland behind my home. But admittedly there are times when I wish that I could keep squirrels off the feeders, and this is not easily accomplished.

One bird feeder that I maintained for chickadees, titmice, nuthatches, woodpeckers, finches, and wrens was relatively free of squirrel problems

for nearly two years, because it was on a deck railing twelve feet above ground level. Then, one winter morning, just as I was about to climb out of bed, there came the soft patter of feet across the roof. This was trouble. One squirrel had finally figured out that it could go around to the front of the house, climb the maple tree, drop to the roof, and cross it. Stationed at the back window, I soon saw it descend a vertical downspout and jump nimbly onto the railing. Thereafter the railing was a squirrel runway leading to the bird feeder. From that day forward, squirrel parties were a regular affair at the feeder anytime during daylight hours. Few birds, even the blue jay, are willing to challenge the gray squirrel as it sits surrounded by sunflower seeds, eating those he chooses and tossing the discards down to the ground.

Another bird feeder that I have since put into operation, however, has frustrated the squirrels. This is a small plastic container shaped like an old-fashioned beehive. Filled with sunflower seeds, it hangs from a fine wire out of jumping range of the squirrels; they stand up like little bears, their heads moving back and forth in time with the swinging feeder as they study the challenging situation.

One might think that a gray squirrel cannot climb a steel pipe, but one would be wrong. After they learned that they could scale the 5 1/2 -foot pipe on which one of my friends maintained a feeder, it was no trick for the squirrels to crawl around the bottom of the feeder and up over the edge to the free-lunch counter. Then the property owner thought of greasing the metal pole with lard. The next squirrel to head for the bird feeder made its usual grand leap at the pole, hit about eighteen inches above the ground, and scrambled for a purchase. For the first time in its experience the squirrel discovered that it could not climb. Instead, it slipped and slid with a thump against the ground. Shaken by this experience, it sat in the snow, looking up at the pole. Then it tried again with identical

results. After four or five tries, it gave up and presumably went sniffing about in the woods for nuts buried the previous autumn.

Also used as a squirrel guard on such poles are large juice cans. Leave both ends in the can and cut an X in the center of each end. Then

Resourceful squirrels often outwit frustrated bird watchers. One solution is to maintain more than one feeding station—including one on a squirrel-proof pole, at least a ten-foot jump from the nearest tree or building.

When all else fails, adjust your attitude and become a squirrel watcher.

Ear corn impaled on nails is relished by squirrels and will help draw them away from feeders.

slide it onto the metal pole to a point high enough to be out of jumping range from the ground. Paint the can when you paint the pole.

One practical way of drawing squirrels away from bird feeders is to offer them ear corn at a respectable distance from where the birds eat. The ears of corn can be impaled on nails driven into a fence post.

Perhaps the most ingenious squirrel-defeating bird feeder available is one that stays open for birds and slams shut in the face of any visiting squirrel. This is made with a weight-balanced platform set to support lightweight birds but not the pound-and-a-half squirrel whose weight depresses the platform, automatically shutting the feeder door. This worked until one of our resident squirrels learned to push open the top and climb into the feeder. Now a small screw secures the lid and, as of this writing, the squirrels have not solved this latest problem.

Any feeder close to trees or other launching platforms is seldom squirrel proof. Squirrels are broad jumpers of considerable ability. But a ten-foot open space discourages them.

Attracting Hummingbirds

An unforgettable high point in a lifetime of bird watching came for me one summer day when I was perhaps twelve years old. The farm wagon on which we were hauling hay to the barn passed under a giant beech tree, and looking up, I saw a small gray cup attached to the top of a low-hanging limb. It was about the same gray as the bark of the beech tree and, although I saw no bird, I knew at once what I had found. This was my first look at a ruby-throated hummingbird's nest, and I returned later after the hay was safely in the barn for a closer look at the nest.

It was coated with lichens that helped camouflage it. I kept my distance and in due time saw one of the parents return to the nest. Many years later these smallest of birds continue to attract my attention whenever I find them, and this fascination with hummingbirds is shared by almost everyone with even the slightest interest in the outdoors. Fortunately, we can tempt the local hummingbirds to come to our flower gardens and feeders. The best way to attract them is to plant a variety of flowers, including those that begin blooming in early spring. In the West, this should bring any of several species of hummingbirds, and in the East, attract the ruby-throated hummingbirds. They come to the flowers to feed on the high-energy nectar. In this mutually beneficial process they are dusted with pollen which they then transport to the next flowers they visit, thereby becoming an instrument in pollination.

In addition, hummingbirds come readily to artificial feeding stations which people provide especially for them. Garden stores and nature shops carry hummingbird feeders in wide variety. Or you can make one with a glass bottle and a rubber stopper with a hole to accommodate a glass tube. Hang this upside down; the vacuum in the top lets the liquid drain out only as fast as the birds drink it.

Hummingbird feeders do not need perches. These smallest of birds hover in front of the flowers from which they extract nectar and they will feed in the same fashion from an artificial feeder. The perch might invite larger birds that keep the hummingbirds away. There is speculation that the hummingbirds need to hover to maintain an optimum body temperature.

Fill one or more of these feeders with sugar water and chances are excellent that the hummingbirds will soon make regular feeding trips to it. The sugar-water mix should consist of four parts water and one part sugar. Bring this to a boil for a couple of minutes then let it cool. Any left over should be refrigerated. Honey is not a good substitute for sugar. There is too much risk that the honey will nurture a mold that kills hummingbirds.

Red is the hummingbird's favorite color. Whether you use food coloring in the solution or not can depend on the feeder. If the feeder is bright red, which many are, the food coloring is probably not needed. If the feeder is clear plastic or glass, you will probably need to add red food coloring to get the birds' attention.

These are a few of the numerous feeders designed to offer sweetened water to hummingbirds.

Cleanliness is essential; the sugar solution spoils, especially during warm summer weather. The feeder should be carefully cleaned with very hot water every couple of days, then refilled. Hummingbirds are highly territorial and will chase each other away from food sources. Several feeders may attract more hummingbirds. Once the visiting birds become accustomed to the locations of feeders, the feeders can be moved closer to windows for better viewing. The hungry birds may even come to second-story windows.

Winter Foods for Wild Birds

Here is a list of foods that will help wild birds live through the winter.

Food	Attracts
Sunflower seed	cardinals, sparrows, pine siskins, grosbeaks, chickadees, titmouse, woodpeckers, blue jays, bobwhites, white-breasted nuthatches, juncos
Millet, wheat	goldfinches, sparrows, purple finches, doves, bobwhites
Oats	mourning doves, bobwhites, ruffed grouse, chickadees
Cracked corn	bobwhites, pheasants, cardinals, chickadees, titmouse, blue jays, nuthatches, ruffed grouse
Shelled corn	pheasants, bobwhites, ruffed grouse, wild turkeys, blue jays, grackles, cardinals
Cracked walnuts	woodpeckers, nuthatches, wrens, blue jays, chickadees, titmouse
Thistle seed	goldfinches, pine siskins
Peanut butter mixtures	titmouse, chickadees, woodpeckers, nuthatches, wrens, blue jays, brown creepers, robins
Sliced apples	wrens, robins, mockingbirds, starlings
Raisins	catbirds, mockingbirds
Bread crumbs	bobwhites, blue jays, chickadees, titmouse, brown creepers, wrens, mockingbirds, robins, starlings, cardinals, juncos, sparrows
Beef suet	woodpeckers, wrens, nuthatches, starlings, chickadees, titmouse, blue jays, brown creepers, mockingbirds

Drinking and Bathing

Birds need water for drinking and for helping them to keep their plumage in condition. Their feather care is vital to the birds' ability to withstand extreme weather and also to fly. Feather condition determines the efficiency of their insulation against the cold.

There are many ways to provide water for birds. Commonly the birdbath is a shallow ceramic bowl or dish on top of a pedestal about three feet high placed in the yard or garden.

Among the simpler birdbaths is one made with a section of tile pipe and the lid from a garbage can. Tie a brick on the lid handle. Set one end of the tile firmly in the ground. Invert the lid on top of the tile with the brick suspended inside the tile to secure the lid in position. Some bird watchers place a large rock in the middle of the lid to anchor it in place. Perhaps the best of all answers to the problem of supplying water for birds, if space permits, is a small pond. If there is room for emergent aquatic vegetation and perhaps a little island in the middle, it will appeal to a wider variety of birds than a simple dish-type birdbath might attract. In addition to providing for the birds, it might also become a watering hole for local raccoons, foxes and other interesting wildlife.

Another favorite watering device is a fountain equipped with a recirculator. Water in motion has a magic attraction for birds. A hose rigged up above a birdbath and turned on just enough to allow water to drip very slowly will bring a variety of birds. Whatever its design, the bird-bath should be a safe place for the birds. The bathing area should be shallow, with no sudden drop-offs. It should be placed in an open area in the sunlight. Nearby escape cover for the birds is helpful, provided there is a clear area enabling them to see any approaching danger.

One way to protect birdbaths from freezing in winter is to equip them with a small submersion-type water heater. Offer only clean water. Adding antifreeze or salt can kill birds.

Cleanliness is important. Wash the bird bath frequently, using hot water with nothing added to it.

Dust Baths

Many birds make occasional use of a dust bath, perhaps as a control measure against parasites. A bird watcher can improve the opportunities for interesting bird observations, and possibly pictures, by providing a place in yard or garden for birds to dust. The dust bath should be in the vicinity of escape cover, but it should still be out in the open where the sun can hit it. It need be nothing big or elaborate, perhaps just an area two or three feet across, kept free of vegetation and providing for visiting birds a mixture of fine sand and earth with which they can shower themselves. Wood ashes are sometimes added to the dust bath. Some suggest treating the area with insecticides. I would disagree. Instead, the visiting birds should be allowed to treat themselves with the same raw materials to which they have become adapted through the centuries.

Problem Birds

Ordinarily a wild animal released in a strange environment perishes. But once in a while there comes an imported creature so adaptable, determined, and pushy that it not only survives but prospers. In this manner America inherited the house sparrow and the European starling. This universal brand of wildlife shuffling has been under way for decades and it is still going on. It is a form of biological pollution that can cause serious consequences ranging from the spreading of foreign wildlife diseases to the direct killing of some native species.

For the benefit of native wildlife it is far kinder to destroy unwanted pet birds from foreign lands than it is to release them, and releasing them may be against the law.

The house sparrows that were brought here from Europe and flock to bird feeders are difficult to discourage. They are seldom a major problem at the feeder where offerings are limited to sunflower seeds, which they do not handle well. But spread millet and other small seeds, and the house sparrows will arrive in force. But so will juncos, white-throated sparrows, house finches, quail, and doves.

Not all trouble-causing birds are of foreign origin. Woodpeckers sometimes make enemies among people who object to the manner in which they use their powerful bills. A Pennsylvania man reported some years ago that he had trouble with a flicker that insisted on chopping holes in the end of his garage. How was this problem met? "I nailed a piece of black garden hose over the garage door," said the flicker victim, "and the bird quit landing on the garage completely. He thought it was a snake."

The biggest of all common woodpeckers, the pileated, sometimes causes problems by drilling into utility poles and buildings. In Columbus, Ohio, one family awakened each morning for a week to a rattle and clatter that sounded as if wreckers had descended upon their dwelling. The commotion was caused by a pileated woodpecker that came shortly after dawn to cut new holes in a window sill. By the end of the

One ornithologist calculates that bird fatalities from collisions with windows number in the millions every year in the United States. Silhouettes of flying owls and hawks on the inside of windows sometimes frighten birds away before they can crash.

week the window was ruined. A new sill was installed, and the woodpecker assault ceased. The homeowner took some comfort from the knowledge that the giant woodpecker had probably detected boring insects in the old sill and was only trying to remove them.

These woodpeckers have also been the subject of serious scientific study by biologists attempting to develop utility poles that would resist woodpecker attacks. In southern Ohio, a utility company spent $13,000 over two years replacing poles weakened by these mighty woodpeckers. Various kinds of metal protection and chemical treatments helped to discourage them.

What do you do when a bird gets into the garage, flutters up to the pitched roof, and dashes itself frantically against wall and window? One family solved the problem by leaving the garage door open, setting a stepladder in the doorway, putting some bird feed on it, then leaving the scene. Eventually the bird calmed down, perched on the ladder, sampled the food, and departed safely.

Occasionally birds turn the tables and attack domestic pets. Blue jays and mockingbirds have been known to make life miserable for family cats and dogs, especially during the birds' nesting season. One Maryland bird watcher reports the case of a tufted titmouse that attacked her cat. The cat, it seems, climbed a tree within the bird's range, and the titmouse dive-bombed the cat, which needed all four feet to hang on to its precarious perch. Then the titmouse found that it could pull hair from the cat. It is said that the diminutive bird even landed on the cat's back, pulled out bits of hair, and darted off to line its nest with the soft material. The cat solved this problem itself when it backed down the tree and departed in ignominious defeat.

One common bird problem is created by the popularity of large picture windows. Birds, seeing sky and clouds reflected in the glass, frequently crash into the windows. The effect on the bird can range from mild shock to sudden death. Even the birds that survive the initial shock are in mortal danger from predators during the recovery period, when they may lie unconscious or immobile on the ground. Our windows have claimed warblers, vireos, thrushes, a yellow-billed cuckoo, and even a barred owl. One answer is a set of black construction-paper silhouettes of owls and crows, fastened to the inside of the window. Such silhouettes are sometimes available commercially from nature-center shops.

Another homeowner, distressed by the number of birds injuring and killing themselves against plate-glass windows, solved the problem by purchasing a plastic great horned owl and placing it on a fence outside the window. Hunters use model owls to attract crows, and consequently these can often be purchased in sporting-goods stores. Decorators' fish net may also be used on the inside.

Long streams of colorful ribbon suspended on the outside of the windows will blow in the breeze and warn approaching birds away from the glass. Meanwhile, curtains drawn across the windows may cut down on reflections and consequently on the bird collisions.

Birds sometimes make themselves unwelcome by feasting on ripening fruit in gardens and orchards. Everyone who grows cherries realizes that he must harvest the fruit before the robins beat him to it. Birds sometimes take the fruit even before it ripens. One Pennsylvania gardener reported that a few rabbit and squirrel skins from the previous year's hunting season, hung high in the cherry trees, caused birds to abandon their raids on the trees, and he speculated that the same effect might be accomplished by using pieces of synthetic fur substitutes.

Scarecrows of various designs have been used for centuries in hopes of frightening birds from strawberries and other crops. The old straw man is still set out, but the effectiveness of this solitary figure is doubtful. One alternative that may be more effective is to suspend strips of aluminum foil from a line strung across the garden. The fragile foil twists in the breezes and reflects the light.

Growers, especially those producing sweet corn and other products in commercial quantities, have turned to noisemakers to discourage the blackbirds from their fields. In late summer, blackbirds form into flocks that in some areas number in the hundreds of thousands. These flocks leave their roosts in early morning, fan out across the country, and settle into the fields of ripening corn to feed on the grain when it is in the milk stage. They strip the husks and ruin much grain. The farmer who doesn't want to switch operations to some less attractive crops can use noisemakers. These generally are carbide guns that explode periodically as they build up charges of gas, causing gunfire-like explosions all through the daylight hours. Neighbors sometimes complain about the noise pollution.

Spring is a bad time to leave garage doors open. If a pair of wrens takes up residence in the garage, the homeowner has only one solution fair to the birds. Leave the door open during the following weeks, rain or shine.

From the state of Washington comes a report of a pair of bluebirds that built a nest in a family mailbox. When the owners first learned of it, they set up an emergency mailbox fashioned from a large tin can and received mail in the tin can until the five bluebird eggs hatched and the young left their mailbox nursery. Before the people could reclaim their mailbox, the bluebirds started a second family in it. But even the mailman did not mind greatly. By this time he had become a bluebird watcher, too.

VI

WHERE TO SEE BIRDS

Eleven Special Vacations

Fortunately, many of the vacation regions that appeal to traveling families because of fine swimming, boating, fishing waters, or exciting wilderness areas to explore also offer excellent opportunities to find, and perhaps photograph, bird species that never before graced the family bird list. The destinations that follow should provide suggestions enough for several years of family travel across this broad and beautiful land. Over the years, we have visited all these regions, and remembered them warmly not alone for their varied bird life but for their scenery and wide range of interesting experiences for the outdoor family. We recommend them for your consideration as you plan another vacation trip.

Upper Mississippi

In the land where the Mississippi River begins, there are forests, fields, and waters providing habitats for birds of many kinds. This north woods region is excellent for those who like to go canoeing. Canoes can slip silently along scenic streams and pleasant lake shores between overnight camps.

In northern Minnesota, the Chippewa National Forest offers the best opportunity

Wild turkey is a spectacular native American bird that has, in recent times, been reintroduced into the woodlands of many states where birders frequently see and hear it. *Luther C. Goldman, U.S. Fish and Wildlife Service.*

between Florida and Alaska for seeing bald eagles in their nesting area. The headquarters of the Chippewa National Forest is at Cass Lake.

Near Holt, Minnesota, is the Agassiz National Wildlife Refuge, set aside by the federal government because of its importance as a nesting area for waterfowl.

Ely, Minnesota, is a major launching area for thousands of canoes that carry visiting paddlers into the famed Border Lakes Canoe Country. Voyageurs National Park, out of International Falls, Minnesota, encompasses more than 217,000 acres of beautiful northern lake and forest country, where the cry of the loon is heard and moose are seen at the water's edge.

Wisconsin has many areas well known among ornithologists for their rich bird life. Do not overlook the Horicon National Wildlife Refuge near Horicon, Wisconsin, Necedah National Wildlife Refuge near the town of the same name, or Lake Koshkonong. Others include Crex Meadows near Grantsburg, the numerous lakes

In autumn, swallows sometimes assemble by the hundreds on convenient utility lines.

and marshes around the capital city of Madison, and the very scenic Baraboo Bluffs region of Sauk County in the vicinity of Leland.

Yellowstone

A remarkable thing about Yellowstone is that no matter how often one has visited this national park there seems to be never a dull moment. The abundance of wild creatures provides a constant show. The spectacular geological features are world-famous. Mud bubbles, boiling water, and white steam issue from the restless earth. Rushing crystal-clear streams and deep-blue lakes are sur-

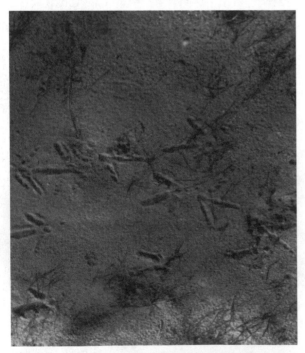

Fresh tracks of the wild turkey are solid evidence that these giants lurk nearby.

they miss a good bit. A few hours on the foot trails can provide a wilderness experience.

Yellowstone is excellent birding country. Bald eagles nest within the park. On the lakes and along the rivers are excellent populations of waterfowl. The trumpeter swan nests here, usually on the smaller mountain ponds. White pelicans float on Yellowstone Lake and have their nesting grounds in the remote areas. There are

The United States has the world's finest system of lands set aside for wildlife. National wildlife refuges are found in every state. Some have self-guided auto trails and observation towers.

rounded by spectacular canyons and mountain vistas draped in lodgepole pines.

Through all this wanders a parade of moose, elk, bison, coyotes, and bears. No wonder this area so impressed early visitors that it became, in 1872, the first of our spectacular national parks.

In addition to bird watching, visitors here can catch cutthroat trout from Yellowstone Lake, hike wilderness trails to remote mountain meadows and streams, camp beneath tall pines, and photograph scenes found nowhere else in the world. By far a majority of Yellowstone's visitors limit their travels about the park to those places their automobile will take them. And

Gulls can often be photographed as they alight on the water to feed, as this one did in Yellowstone National Park.

grebes, sandhill cranes, great blue herons, and California gulls. Magpies, crows, and ravens are commonly seen, and the gray jay, or "camp robber," will come to eat from your picnic table. Watch for the western tanagers, mountain and western bluebirds, and Canada jays. And if you're lucky, you may see the dipper, a short-tailed, sooty-gray bird, about house sparrow size, that specializes in walking under water. The dipper, while wading on the bottom of rushing mountain streams, picks submerged aquatic foods from rock surfaces.

Several parts of Yellowstone are particularly interesting to bird watchers. One of the richest of birding places within the park is marked "Hayden Valley" on your National Park Service map. On a trip through Hayden Valley, you may see Canada geese, trumpeter swans, Barrow's goldeneyes, and white pelicans along the Yellowstone River. No place in the park is better for these wetland species. Here, we stop frequently at the high overlooks to scan the river for ducks, geese, and trumpeter swans. You may also spot a golden eagle, osprey, or red-tailed or Swainson's hawk.

Then pay particular attention to Lamar Valley, a region of spectacular scenery and beautiful little pothole lakes. Watch the lakes for coot and ducks (gadwall, pintail, teal, ring-necked, scaup, ruddy, mallard), as well as sora rails and yellow-headed blackbirds. Along this valley you may also see marsh hawks, golden eagles, cliff swallows, greentailed towhees, Brewer's sparrows, and vesper sparrows. "In the upper reaches of the Absaroka Mountains," says the park naturalist, "watch along the river for dippers, western tanagers, hermit thrushes, mountain chickadees, and Oregon juncos."

The Mammoth area is another special attraction for Yellowstone bird watchers. Follow the Upper Terrace Loop Drive. Pine siskin, mountain chickadee, Clark's nutcracker, mountain bluebird, red-breasted nuthatch, Townsend's solitaire, green-tailed towhee, and blue grouse are good candidates for the bird list here. This corner of the park near Gardiner, incidentally, offers the best possibility for the visitor to see pronghorn antelope. A herd lives in the open rolling hills along the dirt road skirting the edge of the park beyond the old stone gateway, the North Entrance. In this vicinity, also, watch for horned larks and meadowlarks.

If you want to try the foot trails, check first with park rangers about special regulations for backpacking and camping. The Canyon Rim Walk is both scenic and potentially productive, with the promise of bald eagles, ospreys, pine grosbeaks, and Townsend's solitaire. Another hiking possibility with good potential for seeing birds is the Mount Washburn Trail.

This is particularly interesting country for the photographer. When entering Yellowstone, request a copy of the *Birds of Yellowstone National Park,* keep it at hand, and check off new species as you identify them. The ranger can also supply details on current naturalist programs around the park.

Hawaii

Most visitors going to Hawaii limit their visits to the five biggest of the state's islands—Oahu (dominated by Honolulu), Maui, Kauai, Molokai, and Hawaii. Most flights from the mainland arrive and depart by way of Honolulu. Tourists travel between the islands on local airlines. Land transportation for tourists on the islands is mainly by small rental cars available at the airports. There are also tour buses, but these, with their fixed schedules, are seldom satisfactory for people hoping to see some of the island birds.

The bird life of this state is among the world's most interesting. At the time Captain James Cook discovered the Sandwich Islands in 1778, there were at least sixty-nine species of endemic birds found nowhere else in the world. About a third of these are already extinct, another third

This fairy tern comes back to its ancestral island in Hawaii to raise its young.

threatened. But this still leaves birds with such strange-sounding names as apapane, amakihi, and elepaio. Most birds below elevations of two thousand feet, however, are exotics brought in from foreign places and released. They include the cardinal, house sparrow, starling, Japanese white-eye, Chinese dove, mynah, and more.

Each island has its favorite bird haunts. On Oahu these include the Kapiolani Park (the Honolulu Zoo), Aiea Trail, and a drive along the coastal roads. On Hawaii visit Hawaii Volcanoes National Park. Talk with the park naturalist. Maui, among the most beautiful of all islands, has the Haleakala National Park with foot trails winding through the desert country inside the giant caldera of the extinct volcano. On the way up the mountain en route to the park, stop and listen for birds at Hosmer Grove. Kauai has numerous excellent birding places, including the Waimea Canyon, Hawaii's "Grand Canyon."

But as a start purchase a copy of *Hawaii's Birds,* a field guide to the island birds, available from the Hawaii Audubon Society, 212 Merchant St., Suite 320, Honolulu, Hawaii 96813. This booklet includes directions on where to go on each island to see various species of Hawaii's birds.

Outer Banks

Lying between the mainland and the open waters of the Atlantic is a strip of sand that North Carolinians call the Outer Banks. It is a fantastic summertime playground for those who come to walk in the sand, swim in the surf, and camp where they can hear the waves wash themselves out on the beach. For families who want to include bird watching in their vacation trip, the seventy-mile-long Cape Hatteras National Seashore, and surrounding country, is an excellent choice. Along with bird watching you can swim, fish, boat, or collect sea shells. This is the land with something for everyone.

You may wander these beaches and find a tern, nesting where the sands are blowing across the remains of an ancient shipwreck.

The mute swan is a foreign species that, once released, competes with native waterfowl.

Some four hundred species of birds have been recorded along this seashore. Part of the Outer Banks is the famous Pea Island National Wildlife Refuge, covering 5,880 acres, where birders have recorded thirty-four species of shorebirds. From distant parts of North America, waterfowl converge on this area for the winter months. Most spectacular of these birds is the greater snow goose. Thousands of them arrive for the winter, and with them come the Canada geese and many species of ducks, as well as hundreds of whistling swans. This is the site of the only significant nesting population of gadwalls along the Atlantic Coast. Alert bird watchers will also find loons, grebes, herons, egrets, gulls, gannets, rails, vultures, hawks, and perhaps bald eagles. There is a special birding observation point provided on a freshwater pond within the refuge.

The staffs of both the National Seashore and their neighbors at the Pea Island National Wildlife Refuge conduct organized bird programs. Check with them for scheduled events because they know the birds and where to find them.

Unless you plan to go bird watching every hour of the day, take your fishing tackle with you to the Outer Banks. I remember a notable family meal one evening on the sand beach in one of the campgrounds, where the main course was fresh-caught bluefish, cooked in foil over glowing charcoals. There are also mullet, weakfish, or trout, croaker, and red drum in season.

This is photographers' country, with spectacular seascapes, photogenic beach scenes, and birds.

Summers here are somewhat cooler than on the mainland, but light sport clothes are in order. Remember to take precautionary measures against the hot sun, sand, and mosquitoes, which are frequently part of oceanside vacations.

Additional information may be obtained from the headquarters of the Cape Hatteras National Seashore, Manteo, N.C. 27954.

Florida

Florida is one of the world's richest areas in bird life. Books have been written about the birds of Florida, and still others will be. Here, in various seasons, one may find species he cannot find anywhere else in the country. Keeping a Florida bird list becomes an excellent project for any family planning a Florida vacation.

In south Florida, the Florida Keys is an exciting region, with great white herons, egrets, pelicans, man-o'-war birds, and many more. On Big Pine Key, the Key Deer National Wildlife Refuge harbors a remarkable population of small birds often overlooked by those who stop

This mixture of gulls, terns, and cormorants was photographed by a birder visiting Cedar Key National Wildlife Refuge on the Gulf coast of Florida.

Roseate spoonbill is a favorite with bird listers visiting Everglades National Park.

in to see the tiny white-tailed deer for which this area is famous.

Everglades National Park is a magnificent area for everyone. Waiting for travelers who can arrange a winter vacation are birds down from the North to mingle with the year-round residents. Traveling to or from Flamingo, I always check Mrazek Pond. If you are there at the right time, this pond offers an unforgettable collection of birds. I arrived one morning shortly after dawn to find roseate spoonbills, egrets, skimmers, great white herons, and more, crowding onto the pond to feed. A flock of white pelicans, in Florida for the winter, soon arrived and began herding small fish into the shallows and scooping them up in bulk. Furthermore, all were within good range for pictures. At Flamingo there is an excellent campground and a good motel, but it is a good idea to pack your own lunch.

If you particularly like to list rare and endangered species, try to arrange a trip out onto Lake Okeechobee from a marina on the northern part of the lake. Some marina operators know the location of the rare Everglades kite. This bird, like birds everywhere, should not be molested or closely approached during the nesting season.

Out of Naples is the National Audubon Society's famed Corkscrew Swamp, a remnant virgin cypress swamp and a famous refuge for the wood ibis or wood stork, the only true stork in North America. This is another endangered species you can add to your list.

Sanibel Island, famed for birds and seashells, is on this Gulf Coast side of Florida. A large part of the island, which is reached by a causeway out of Ft. Myers, lies within the J.N. "Ding" Darling National Wildlife Refuge. Watch for black skimmers, ruddy turnstones, mottled ducks, gray kingbirds, and many others.

While you are in the Tallahassee area, take time to visit Wakulla Springs, where commercially operated boats carry visitors onto the crystal-clear waters of the Wakulla River, close to good populations of limpkins, waterfowl, and other species. In this part of Florida, also, visit the seventy-thousand-acre St. Marks National Wildlife Refuge, with its remarkable and varied

Shallow waters of a pond in Everglades National Park become a concentration area for egrets, ducks, herons, and other birds flocking in, at dawn, to harvest their natural foods. Visitors fortunate enough to be there at the right time can list several species from a single location.

National Audubon Society maintains numerous important refuges including Corkscrew Swamp Sanctuary near Naples, Florida. The boardwalk makes it easy for birders to reach the heart of the sanctuary.

population of birds. Here one may find long-billed marsh wrens, seaside sparrows, willets, redbellied woodpeckers, and outstanding wintering populations of ducks and geese. The Merritt Island National Wildlife Refuge at Cape Canaveral is another outstanding area for birds and birders. I always allow time here to drive the auto trail around the area because it seems always to hold surprises for birders.

Florida birders will say this is only the beginning of a list of that state's good bird-watching areas. They are right, of course.

Great Smoky Mountains National Park

No national park in the country attracts more visitors year after year than this timbered mountain wonderland in the Great Smoky Mountains. The park reaches fifty-four miles from east to west and is fifteen miles wide from north to south. Elevations range up to 6,643 feet at Clingmans Dome, and the range of life zones lends variety to the plant life and bird species. Those who want to get out and hike can choose from six hundred miles of trails. There are more than six hundred miles of streams, most of them small ones, flowing down out of the wooded hollows.

Botanists, even more than ornithologists, find this a remarkable area. There are more than 1,300 kinds of flowering plants found within the Great Smoky Mountains National Park, 350 mosses and liverworts, and, according to longtime park naturalist Arthur Stupka, 230 kinds of lichens. There are more than 100 kinds of trees native to the park, many of them of record sizes.

Those who venture into the highest parts of the Great Smokies around Clingmans Dome will find such Canadian-zone nesting birds as golden-crowned kinglets, saw-whet owls, brown creepers, winter wrens, and red-breasted nuthatches. The hoarse call of the raven can be heard in the high places, and because the raven

is one of my favorite birds, this is reason enough to return to the Great Smoky Mountains. In this high country birders also listen for the notes of warblers that they might otherwise have to travel to Canada to hear.

The park headquarters, near Gatlinburg, is an important early stop for visitors searching for the park's wildlife. Excellent publications available at the Park Service Book Shop provide detailed descriptions of the birds to be found in this mountain region. Arthur Stupka's *Notes on the Birds of Great Smoky Mountains National Park* is especially valuable.

If time and the direction of travel make it practical, it is an excellent plan to extend the trip to include all or part of the Blue Ridge Parkway where motorists cruise at a leisurely pace, free of the pressures of traffic lights and commercial trucks. This scenic drive, administered by the National Park Service, follows the mountain ridges for some five hundred miles through the southern Appalachians.

Alaska

Few places on this continent, or any continent, have populations of birds to rival those that live in Alaska at some time during the year. Millions of waterfowl hatch in the Yukon Flats, the North Slope, and elsewhere in this giant state. The long-tailed jaeger arrives each year from islands near Japan. The wheatear, having spent the winter in Asia, returns to Alaska to nest. Meanwhile, sea birds funnel in to the dark cliffsides of the Gulf shore islands to nest side by side, by the hundreds of thousands. Among them are auklets, murres, and puffins. Trumpeter swans hatch their gray fluffy cygnets on tiny ponds in forest and tundra, while magnificent bald eagles with flashing white tails and heads soar above the seacoast.

This, and more, makes Alaska a once-in-a-lifetime vacation destination for all those interested in the out of doors. The only problem

Emperor goose on nest in Alaska.

comes in trying to reach those Alaskan areas richest in wildlife. The larger part of the state is still a wilderness untouched by highways. The airplane becomes the common mode of transportation. Small charter planes are often the major link between remote communities and the outside world. But planes and chartered boats still reach a surprisingly large number of Alaskan destinations. There is even regular service to the far north villages of Kotzebue, Nome, and Barrow.

There is, however, much to see from the highways. If you are driving to Alaska, consider making part of the trip by water on the Marine Highway. State-owned ferries provide passage for passengers and vehicles alike through the beautiful forested islands and the fiords of southeastern Alaska's timber country. Here lives the greatest remaining concentration of bald eagles anywhere. From here the road leads to Fairbanks, then south to Anchorage, with Denali National Park and Preserve between these major cities. A single road, most of it unsurfaced, leads into the

park. Private cars are prohibited except for the first fourteen miles. Instead, visitors ride tour buses or the yellow shuttle buses provided by the Park Service. In peak tourist seasons, visitors must sometimes wait a day or two for space on the shuttle buses. But it is worth the wait because of the chance of seeing North America's highest peak, Mt. McKinley—or, as the native people call it, "Denali"—the high one. Even when clouds obscure the peak, you will probably see grizzly bears, Dall sheep, caribou, moose, and perhaps a wolf.

The most recent visit we made to Denali produced a bird list including golden eagle, Say's phoebe, long-tailed jaeger, raven, willow ptarmigan, white-crowned sparrow, and a brief glimpse of a little brown job that still puzzles me. There are kinglets, Hudsonian curlews, wandering tattlers, surfbirds, Lapland longspurs, and snow buntings. All things considered, label Denali "unforgettable."

Prince William Sound is another Alaskan destination famous among birders. If you want to add seabirds to your list, plan a day cruise out of Seward or Valdez. The boat captains often know the birds well and point out horned and tufted puffins, common murres, pigeon guillemots, and others. On a rainy day out of Seward, when dark clouds obscured the towering mountains flanking Resurrection Bay, and foul weather cut the trip in half, we still saw enough birds to make this a memorable trip.

From Juneau the traveler can reach Glacier Bay National Monument by airplane or boat but not by highway. Here, in addition to spectacular glaciers, travelers see geese, cormorants, loons, gulls, terns, murrelets, guillemots, puffins, ducks, bald eagles, shorebirds, ravens, and ptarmigan.

There are good paved roads out of Anchorage and southward toward Kenai and Homer, which also offer excellent bird-watching opportunities. In Homer there is an excellent opportunity to add shorebirds to the bird list.

Common murre is an ocean-going fishing bird that nests on rock ledges of seaside cliffs. These murres were photographed in Alaska.

Twenty-four species of shorebirds have been identified here. From the Homer Spit the birder may also spot seabirds, ducks, and eiders of various species.

The Pribilof Islands offer an unforgettable birding experience. The cliffs are decorated with unbelievable numbers of seabirds. There are scheduled flights to the Pribilofs. Expensive though.

In recent years the tourist traffic to Alaska has grown. Early reservations are important. The best months are June, July, and August. Write Division of Tourism, P.O. Box 110801, Juneau, Alaska 99811-0801 for additional information.

Desert Country

Traveling in the deserts of the Southwest can be richly rewarding for birders. In one trip through the Southwest we visited four of the better-known desert parks and monuments, beginning with Death Valley. Today this dry region of stark mountain landscapes is less formidable than the name implies. Hundreds of thousands of people now flock to Death Valley each year. The best time is winter. Summer can become unbearably hot, with thermometers rising to 120° in the shade. Winter is also one of the better times for bird finding in Death Valley. More than 230 species have been recorded here. Alert black ravens soar over the valleys. In winter the phainopepla lives here, and among the summer residents are the hairy woodpecker, gray flycatcher, rock wren, mountain bluebird, Cooper's hawk, poor-will, California jay, and others.

Death Valley National Monument, 140 miles long by about 16 miles wide, reaches north and south between ranges of towering multicolored mountains. To the east are the Grapevine, Funeral, and Black mountains, while on the west the valley is flanked by the Panamint, Cottonwood, and Last Chance mountains. Elevations range from 282 feet below sea level, the lowest on the North American continent, to 11,049 feet at Telescope Peak. In those years when heavy winter rains fall on Death Valley, spring brings a splendid display of wild flowers to carpet the dry slopes.

The Death Valley National Monument headquarters is at Furnace Creek.

About two hundred miles to the south, near Twentynine Palms, is Joshua Tree National Monument. The odd-shaped Joshua trees, which give this area its name, are really a species of giant lily growing thirty feet high or more and living sometimes for two hundred years. This is a wonderland. Scenic landscapes are filled with giant rock formations. Trails lead off into the deserts. Birds listed among the winter visitors include the gray flycatcher, sage thrasher, and Brewer's sparrow.

From Interstate 10, Highway 62 leads north toward the main entrance to the monument east of Twentynine Palms. A stop at the monument headquarters is an excellent beginning for a visit to this desert area. This national monument, covering more than half a million acres, includes portions of both the Colorado and Mojave deserts and extends from elevations of near sea level to more than five thousand feet.

Another remarkable desert area just outside Tucson, Arizona, is Saguaro National Monument, considered by many to be the world's most spectacular natural cactus garden. Here you may add to your bird list such species as the gila woodpecker, gilded flicker, elf owl, and cactus wren.

Organ Pipe Cactus National Monument, home of the rare giant cactus from which it takes its name, is on the Mexican border west of Tucson. It is reached by driving down Highway 85 from Interstate 8. About thirty kinds of cacti thrive here. Take along camping equipment and, of course, the cameras.

Grand Canyon

For 217 miles the roaring Colorado River has carved its mile-deep gorge across northern Arizona. In the process it has cut down through 2 billion years of the earth's history. There are three worlds of the Grand Canyon, each offering different species of plants and animals. The most heavily visited is the South Rim. Here people walk the nature trails and look into the depths of the canyon.

This is also the starting point for another and more rigorous visit to Grand Canyon by foot trail or mule. (To make the mule trip, write well in advance to Fred Harvey, Grand Canyon, Ariz. 86023.) Descending into the canyon, you see the layered rocks revealing the story of the earth's formation.

The story of the Grand Canyon is the story of life zones with different temperatures, plants, and animals, grading from one zone to the next as you travel to the bottom of the canyon or back to its rim. Five of these life zones are represented in the canyon at elevations ranging from two thousand to nine thousand feet. This means a wide variety of plants and animals. At the river level you may encounter the black-throated sparrow known to the Lower Sonoran zone but not found on the rim. Each bird is more or less related to its own zone, and the Grand Canyon is an excellent compact demonstration of this phenomenon.

The third world of Grand Canyon is the North Rim, some one thousand feet higher than the South Rim and nine miles from it across the canyon. Many visitors favor this approach. The road leads through beautiful forests of Douglas fir, aspen, and ponderosa pine, with green alpine meadows famous for their deer, wild turkeys, and other wildlife. Here are birds of the alpine forests, such species as Clark's nutcracker, brown creeper, golden-crowned and ruby-crowned kinglets, and the evening grosbeak.

Hiking and mule trips to the river can also be started from this spectacular North Rim by way of the North Kaibab Trail.

Whooping Crane Country

A winter trip to the southern tip of Texas and the Gulf Coast can add many new species to the life list of most non-Texans. One of my first targets in that area is always the Aransas National Wildlife Refuge, made famous by the whooping cranes. Each autumn they wing 2,500 miles down across the continent from the wilderness bogs of the Northwest Territories to this ancestral wintering area along the Gulf Coast. They spend these months between November and April on or close to the sprawling national wildlife refuge, which is reached by driving narrow roads through cotton country out of Austwell, Texas.

Wildlife biologist shows visiting birders where the wintering whooping cranes feed on Aransas National Wildlife Refuge.

Visitors coming to see the whooping cranes, and other wildlife, encounter this sign at the refuge entrance.

Top: Birders searching for whooping cranes from deck of the tour boat. *Below:* This boat, operating out of Rockwell, Texas, carries hundreds of visiting birders into the whooping crane's wintering area. *Right:* Heron at boundary of National Audubon Society sanctuary in south Texas.

There is an observation tower on the refuge, and on occasion, visitors see whoopers from this vantage point. They will also record numerous other species, including caracara and scissortailed flycatchers.

Although you may catch a glimpse of whooping cranes in the distance from the refuge, the more certain way to get close to them is by boat. Start at Rockport at the Sea Gun Inn, where the M.V. *Whooping Crane* is docked. This tour boat makes frequent trips daily up the channel and into the territories of the whoopers during fall and winter.

Then, while you are in south Texas, remember two other famed birding areas which, like Aransas, are national wildlife refuges, main-

tained by the federal government. One is Santa Ana, west of Brownsville. Write to the Manager, Santa Ana Lower Rio Grande Valley Complex, 320 N. Main, Rm. A-103, McAllen, TX 78501. This refuge on the Rio Grande has a flock of easily viewed chachalaca, which moved out of the shaded dirt road reluctantly the last time I drove through the area. The bird list on this area of less than two thousand acres totals 272 species. Bird watchers come to this refuge from distant points to see its birds.

Equally famous is the Laguna Atascosa National Wildlife Refuge, with a bird list of 317 species. The address of this one is P.O. Box 450, Rio Hondo, TX 78583.

Near Mission, Texas, is Bentsen-Rio Grande

Luther C. Goldman, U.S. Fish and Wildlife Service.

Among the rarest and most famous birds are these towering white whooping cranes that nest in the Canadian wilderness and winter on the Texas coast.

W. F. Kubichek, U.S. Fish and Wildlife Service.

Valley State Park which is famous for rare and unusual birds. In addition there is the Padre Island National Seashore, with shore birds, gulls, terns, waterfowl, and numerous others. This vacation area offers a full schedule for birding families.

Platte—River of Cranes

If you want to take a strictly birding vacation and see a sky full of birds—big ones—plan an early spring trip to Nebraska's Platte River country when the lesser sandhill cranes are on the scene. Through March and early April each year these three-foot-tall birds arrive by the hundreds of thousands in the forty-five-mile stretch of the Platte River between Kearney and Grand Island.

In these weeks, most of the world's total population of half a million lesser sandhills crowd into the Platte River area and bring birders from every state and several foreign lands. Nowhere else can they see this many cranes gathered within easy viewing distance. The numbers are difficult to count or estimate as the flocks layer the sky and move across the setting sun, but I feel confident that I've seen fifteen thousand or more sandhills here in a single evening.

The best views are from established bird blinds maintained for visiting birders. Near Grand Island there is an observation point maintained by the Platte River Whooping Crane Habitat Maintenance Trust, 2550 North Diers Avenue, Grand Island 68803. Blinds are also maintained by the National Audubon Society's Lillian Annette Rowe Sanctuary, Rt. 2, Box 1120A, Gibbon, Nebraska 68840. It is a good idea to make reservations as soon after January 1 as possible because, year after year, the number of crane watchers keeps growing.

Cranes come to the Platte from their wintering areas in the southwestern United States and Mexico, and they are on their way to nesting grounds in Northern Canada, Alaska, and Siberia. But that is a long flight. The Nebraska stopover gives them the opportunity to store up energy for the remainder of their trip to the Far North.

The Platte River Valley is important to the migrating cranes for several reasons. Here they can glean grain dropped in the fields by the farmers' harvesting machines. They can supplement this with high-protein animal matter in the form of worms and other small organisms gathered from the wet meadows.

Then, when night comes, the sandhills find the river itself an attractive roosting place. They sleep standing in shallow water on one foot. Surrounded by their moat, they are relatively safe from mammalian predators.

The best crane-watching hours are daybreak and sunset. As daylight comes to the Platte River country, flocks of the birds lift off from their roosting places in the river and head for the surrounding fields to begin feeding. In late evening they return by the thousands. The air is filled with cranes and the cacophony of their trumpeting calls.

Watch as well for the bald eagles that perch in the tops of the cottonwood trees, and for the ducks which pass through this area in large numbers. There may even be an occasional towering white whooping crane mingling with the sandhill cranes.

In these early weeks of spring, bitter winds sometimes sweep across Nebraska and crane watchers should take along down jackets, gloves, and warm footgear.

Birding by States

Every corner of the continent has its interesting birds for those who would go searching for them. In the following pages we have tried to list the more productive bird-watching areas in each state. Others could be added in every case. You may already know of good places we've missed in these brief roundups, and if so that is your good fortune. The information here has been checked and obtained by local people intimately acquainted with the regions, members of Audubon societies, professional wildlife biologists of state and federal governments, university staff people, and park and nature-center supervisors who have generously shared, with birders everywhere, these tips on where to find birds.

Alabama

The Gulf Coast provides the most exciting bird watching in Alabama. This is especially true from mid-April to May and again from mid-August to mid-December. Dauphin Island is particularly outstanding during these migration times. Also noteworthy is the causeway by which U.S. 90 crosses Mobile Bay.

Experienced Alabama birders point to the Fred T. Stimpson Game Sanctuary near Jackson as a top spot in their state. This sanctuary lies in the coastal plains section of Alabama. Its varied habitat types include both upland and the lowland areas embracing large swamps and helps to account for the large numbers of birds and the impressive list of species. Among the nesting birds that might be seen on this refuge are wild turkeys, as well as Mississippi and swallow-tailed kites.

Another excellent Alabama location is the Choctaw National Wildlife Refuge.

On the eastern side of the state visit the Eufaula National Wildlife Refuge, which is considered especially good for winter bird watching. January brings hundreds of people to Guntersville State Park where, in recent times, large numbers of bald eagles have concentrated on Lake Guntersville in midwinter. Eagle watchers come from around the country, and other countries as well, to see the birds and participate in the special programs.

Meanwhile, in north-central Alabama, bird watchers consider Cheaha State Park to be a special attraction in spring.

Little River State Park, near Fort Payne, in the northeastern part of Alabama, is another rewarding stop.

Also in the northern part of the state is Wheeler National Wildlife Refuge, established on part of a TVA reservoir and rich in wildlife, especially during fall and winter months when geese and ducks congregate here by the thousands.

Alaska

(See page 154)

Arizona

Those who enjoy the study of birds discover exciting country in Arizona's deserts and splendid mountains. Among the more popular visitor areas is Saguaro National Monument, in the southern part of the state. The giant cactus for which this area is named is found in no other desert in the world. Its towering, fluted columns are home to a variety of birds. Northern flickers and gila woodpeckers dig into the fleshy arms of the saguaro and hollow out nesting areas for themselves. Fluids within the plant then harden and form a tough, dry lining in the cavities. Old cavities become nesting areas for American kestrels, elf owls, screech owls, brown-crested flycatchers, and purple martins. White-winged doves are frequently seen nesting on the arms of the saguaro cactus. The large, noisy cactus wren and the black-throated sparrow are found here. This is only a beginning. Stop at the monument headquarters and pick up a bird list. While in Tucson take time to visit the Arizona-Sonora Desert Museum.

Out of Patagonia, also in the southern part of the state, and not far north of the Mexican border, is Sonoita Creek, a favorite birding area for Arizona residents and visitors. Among the birds to be recorded here are canyon towhees, ground-doves, acorn woodpeckers, and Bewick's wren.

Another highly productive bird-watching area is the Verde Valley. Near Camp Verde there are large areas of cottonwoods, which harbor a spectacular number of nesting birds in summer as well as migrants in winter. Within this valley also are Peck's Lake and Tavasci Marsh, both important to the serious birder.

Another area of this river-valley habitat considered extremely productive by Arizona birders is found along the famed Oak Creek Canyon, all the way from Pumphouse Wash to Sedona. This area, south of Flagstaff, harbors a wide variety of birds, including the painted redstart, western tanager, and black-headed grosbeak.

In the Flagstaff vicinity, Mormon Lake, which is reached by Highway 487, south of town, often provides the opportunity to see waterfowl.

Organ Pipe Cactus National Monument on the Mexican border south of Ajo on Highway 85 is a large and beautiful desert region with a wide variety of strange plants and a good population of birds, including such species as greater roadrunner, northern flicker, verdin, and phainopepla.

Much of Arizona's finest birding is found in the southern part of the state. This is the area that provides excellent opportunities for adding new species, especially near the International Boundary where ranges of northern and southern species overlap. Permanent rivers and creeks with stands of tall trees and brushy understory are best of all and have been the focal situation for much of Arizona's outstanding bird watching. Next come the marshes and swamps. But much of Arizona is dry and thirsty. In such areas sewage-settling ponds may attract large populations of migrating birds, and in these locations Arizona bird watchers have recorded some of their rarest shorebirds and water birds.

Arkansas

Waterfowl hunters have known for decades that the lowlands draining into the Mississippi and its tributaries along the eastern side of Arkansas are host to one of the world's most concentrated waterfowl populations in autumn and winter months. Likewise, these lands provide wintering areas for smaller birds of forest and field that come down from northern areas.

The Arkansas Game and Fish Commission has managed extensive wildlife areas, particularly on the state's national forest lands, and these management areas support good bird populations. They can be located by consulting the state wildlife officers in county-seat towns or the Arkansas Game and Fish Commission in Little Rock. Ask about the Piney Creeks Wildlife Management Area and other such areas, including Muddy Creek, Sylamore, Winona, Caney Creek, and St. Francis. The state has a total of about sixty-four such wildlife management areas. Each includes a wilderness area of forty or more acres.

West of Fayetteville is Lake Weddington, well

known to Arkansas birders for its abundance of wintering waterfowl. The uplands around the lake have populations of typical woodland birds.

Also reached out of Fayetteville is Devils Den State Park, densely wooded hill country especially good for woodland species. South of Stuttgart is the Bayou Meto Wildlife Management Area, also considered one of Arkansas's finest areas for wildlife. For waterfowl and shorebirds visit the state fish hatcheries near Lonoke and Hot Springs.

Arkansas birders should visit the White River National Wildlife Refuge east of Stuttgart. Begin by checking with the staff at refuge headquarters in DeWitt. The flooded river-bottom hardwoods here are a haven for migrating and wintering waterfowl, and in summer there are nesting herons, anhingas, black-crowned night herons, and wood ducks.

Holla Bend National Wildlife Refuge, Russellville, Arkansas, has a bird list of more than 140 species and a variety of habitat types. Visitors to Holla Bend may see ducks, geese, and herons as well as bobwhites and other upland species. Other National Wildlife Refuges, all of them excellent birding locations, include Big Lake near Manila, Felsenthal near Crossett, and Wapanocca near Turrell.

California

California offers some of the most spectacular bird watching anywhere, and in all seasons. In the northern part of the Central Valley, Sacramento National Wildlife Refuge, out of Willows, for example, is the wintering area for a million or more pintails, mallards, widgeon, snow, white-fronted, and cackling geese along with other waterfowl and thousands of shorebirds. The big concentrations are here from fall to late winter, reaching peak numbers in December.

"In autumn, Mono Lake," says one California biologist, "is fantastic" for eared grebes, Wilson's phalaropes, California gulls and others. In summer there is excellent waterfowl viewing at Salton Sea National Wildlife Refuge, northeast of San Diego, which may attract visiting birds from the south following their breeding season in nearby Mexico. But the large numbers concentrate here for the winter months, while songbirds pass through in spring and fall.

In the northern part of the state are Tule Lake and Lower Klamath National Wildlife Refuges, famous for concentrations of migrating waterfowl as well as raptors or birds of prey.

All this boils down to the fact that California offers more fine birding areas than most people ever visit. The coastline has cormorants, gulls, grebes, loons, terns, and more. The mountains have sparrows, kinglets, mountain quail, and raptors. In the deserts you may add to your list the roadrunner, Gambel's quail, Costa's hummingbird, cactus wren, turkey vulture, and many more.

California has numerous publicly owned areas, both state and federal, noted for their birds. As one California birder summed it up for me, "There are hundreds of places that could be included." In Yosemite, Sequoia, Joshua Tree, Lassen Volcanic, Kings Canyon, and Death Valley national parks and monuments, inquire of the park naturalists for the best current information on birding opportunities.

The California Department of Fish and Game, 1416 Ninth Street, Sacramento 95814, has an active "Watchable Wildlife" program that identifies key wildlife viewing areas. Numerous state parks are among the favorite California birding locations.

There are several recent detailed guides to birding in California which are available in nature shops and bookstores.

Colorado

With its five life zones, Colorado boasts a wide variety of bird life. Skilled ornithologists, amateur and professional, have scoured the corners of Colorado for many years, and all the better birding areas in the state are well known to them. When I asked the late Dr. Alfred M. Bailey, for many years director of the Denver Museum of Natural History, for his favorite Colorado birding areas, he led off with Rocky Mountain National Park.

There is, of course, more than birds to attract visitors to this fantastic scenic region, with its snow-capped mountain peaks, deep-blue mountain pools, and alpine wildflower gardens. The bird list here totals some 260 species, and one of the best ways to see a wide variety of them is to travel the famous Trail Ridge Road as it extends from the lower reaches of the park into the tundra and passes through four life zones. Summer visitors may find horned larks, water pippets, and other tundra species on their nesting grounds. There are fine hiking trails within this park, and they lead to trout streams as well as to the haunts of birds.

Another high-country target area for the bird watcher is a trip up Mount Evans on the highest paved road in the United States, elevation 14,264 feet. Here you can pass through five different life zones and consequently encounter, with careful search, many of the birds found throughout the state. This area is reached by traveling west from Denver on I-70. Experienced birders visiting this area will want to search for the brown-capped rosy finch, a potential new addition to many a life list.

In northeastern Colorado, there are in the Fort Collins/Greeley area a number of lakes which attract waterfowl and other birds, particularly during migration seasons.

Following Highway 14 west out of Fort Collins will bring one to the forested mountains and Chambers Lake, in a valley of green meadows and beaver ponds where the Laramie River rises. Also in this corner of Colorado is the Pawnee National Grassland. Summer finds the prairie species nesting through this area, among

them the Lapland longspur, lark bunting, horned lark, western meadowlark, and grasshopper sparrow. The total bird list here includes some two hundred species. This is an excellent area to view golden eagles and other birds of prey. Briggsdale, northeast of Greeley, lies in the heart of this grassland.

A region considered excellent birding country by Colorado naturalists is the San Luis Valley, which includes two national wildlife refuges, Monte Vista and Alamosa, as well as the Great Sand Dunes National Monument. In this region do not overlook the birding possibilities around the San Luis Lake, north of Alamosa, or Russell Lakes. There should be shorebirds, raptors, waterfowl, and numerous others, including sandhill cranes, as well as typical prairie species.

Connecticut

In southeastern Connecticut, visit the Barn Island Wildlife Management Area east of Stonington. There are salt marshes, mixed hardwoods, abandoned farm fields, and open salt water. Says the Connecticut Department of Environmental Protection, "The entire area provides excellent birding." Winter brings waterfowl to the bay, while shorebirds come in spring and fall.

Near Hampton the James L. Goodwin State Forest is considered by local birders to be a top area. Nature trails make hiking easy. The forest headquarters has maps and guide books available.

Natchaug State Forest, near Phoenixville, is known for its wide variety of habitat and bird species. Northeast of Norwich, near Voluntown, lies the Pachaug State Forest, with a fine grove of rhododendron and a white cedar swamp. Forest roads and foot trails lead through marshes, fields, and timberlands.

Near Sharon is the excellent Sharon Audubon Center, maintained by the National Audubon Society. There are frequent bird hikes scheduled here and an excellent trailside museum.

Delaware

Members of the Delmarva Ornithological Society pass along suggestions on their favorite birding places in Delaware. Around the capital city of Wilmington two areas are considered particularly productive. One is the Alapocas Woods County Park. Another is Brandywine Creek State Park.

In the vicinity of Delaware City pay a visit to Dragon Run Marsh.

The Bombay Hook National Wildlife Refuge on Delaware Bay, near Smyrna, is top-quality birding country in any season. There is a twenty-five-mile auto tour route as well as observation towers and hiking trails. This is a good place to see a wide variety of waterfowl, shorebirds, and wading birds during seasons of migration and nesting.

Broadkill Beach is also good bird country, and while traveling to and from the beach watch closely for birds along the road.

Another prominent birding location is Cape Henlopen near Lewes. And in the Rehoboth area take time to visit Gordon's Pond, the Indian River Inlet, and Rehoboth Bay. Scientists have found that this whole coastal area is a vitally important area for shorebirds stopping over in their migrations as well as for migrating songbirds and the raptors that follow them. If parts of the beaches are closed seasonally, this is to protect the birds at the critical times when they are feeding, resting and, in some instances, nesting.

In addition to these popular locations, if time and opportunity permit, search the Assawoman Wildlife Area and Little Creek Wildlife Area.

The Delmarva Peninsula, however, is divided among three states, Delaware, Maryland, and Virginia, and these Delaware locations bring the visitor close to other outstanding peninsula wildlife areas, including Assateague Island National Seashore and Chincoteague National Wildlife Refuge. The peninsula attracts remarkably large populations of birds during the periods of migration and through the summer as well, and is one of the major birding areas of the east.

Florida

(See page 151)

Georgia

Okefenokee National Wildlife Refuge, in Georgia, is a unique area, rich in wildlife and a remarkable variety of wetland vegetation. Nesting here are sandhill cranes and the endangered red-cockaded woodpecker. Start by visiting refuge headquarters at Waycross or the visitor's center at Camp Cornelia. Another national wildlife refuge not to be overlooked is Savannah, with headquarters at Box 8487, Savannah, Georgia 31402. It has a bird list of more than two hundred species.

Georgia has numerous state wildlife areas established primarily for hunting but also well

The anhinga is a fishing bird that sometimes swims with only its head and neck out of the water. These birds were photographed in Okenfenokee National Wildlife Refuge.

Red-winged blackbirds in Okenfenokee National Wildlife Refuge in southern Georgia use lily pads for landing mats.

known to local bird watchers. These wildlife management areas are to be found from the seacoast and lower coastal plains to the mountaintops of north Georgia. The coastal areas usually produce the greatest numbers of individuals and species. The Georgia Department of Natural Resources can supply a list of its wildlife management areas. Among those wildlife management areas considered by Georgia bird watchers to be especially productive are Allatoona, Berry College, Cedar Creek, Ocmulgee, Arabia Bay, Brunswick, and Altamaha.

The Georgia Department of Natural Resources encourages visitors to its game management areas to start by consulting conservation officers in county-seat towns.

Off the coast of Georgia are a number of islands with interesting wildlife populations.

Blackbeard Island National Wildlife Refuge can be reached by boat while a good highway leads to Tybee Island.

Hawaii
(See page 148)

Idaho
When he was asked for the location of Idaho's top bird-watching areas, one employee of the Fish and Game Department confidently answered, "anywhere." Though this may be true, the fact remains that some parts of the "anywhere" are better than others. Idaho is a magnificent, big state of forest, mountains, and deep wilderness. Its variety of topography,

weather, and climate between the lower valleys and higher mountains makes it the home of water birds, forest birds, and desert species as well as those to be found in the irrigated valley. In just about any part of Idaho you choose to visit, there should be excellent possibilities of seeing some of the 280 species of birds on this state's list.

The Idaho Fish and Game Department maintains a number of wildlife management areas, primarily for hunting and fishing. There are also some two hundred access areas managed by this department and enabling public access to lands that would otherwise not be readily visited. These areas are marked by signs. Maps of the wildlife management areas are available from the Fish and Game Department, 600 South Walnut, P.O. Box 25, Boise, Idaho 83707. These are, of course, published primarily for hunters and fishermen whose money established the public areas.

There are also in Idaho a number of excellent public areas in national wildlife refuges. Five miles northwest of Hamer is the 10,500-acre Camas National Wildlife Refuge, where one is likely to see migrating tundra swans, a variety of ducks, Canada geese, sage grouse, pheasants, and longbilled curlews, to name a few.

Deer Flat National Wildlife Refuge, near Nampa, is the home and migration stop of Canada geese, ducks, white pelicans, gulls, and others. By mid-November, migrating ducks may number three quarters of a million on this refuge.

Minidoka National Wildlife Refuge, near Rupert, covers 25,600 acres and is also primarily a waterfowl refuge.

A visit to Bear Lake in Southeast Idaho can turn up a variety of waterfowl, shorebirds, and other wetland species.

Backpackers who want to go by foot into wilderness or primitive areas will find plenty of excellent hiking country in the Idaho mountains. There are trails that lead to fine little mountain lakes and rushing streams. These can make for an excellent combination of fishing, bird watching, and hiking vacation for those who carry pack rods and reels, along with bird guide and binoculars. These areas are managed primarily by the U.S. Forest Service, which can supply detailed trail maps and information from its district offices.

Illinois

Experienced bird watchers in Illinois consider the southern part of the state to be more productive than the northern part. One experienced ornithologist listing his favorite Illinois birdwatching areas puts Crab Orchard National Wildlife Refuge at the top. This waterfowl area, near Carbondale, covers 44,000 acres and includes a 7,000-acre lake with 125 miles of shoreline. Large numbers of waterfowl come here to spend the winter months. Canada geese are abundant in this season. Visitors by the thousands watch the migrating waterfowl in autumn. The bird list for the area includes more than 234 species, 100 of them known to be breeding residents.

Shawnee National Forest is another favorite birding location with the Pine Hills-LaRue Swamp area being excellent. Here birders search the sandstone bluffs and swamp habitat that lies parallel to the Mississippi River. The location is near Grand Tower, Illinois. Beall Woods is a remnant virgin forest near Mount Carmel and a good bird-watching area in the southern part of the state.

Illinois has numerous state areas classified either as parks, conservation areas, or state forests. The avian ecologist of the Department of Conservation's Division of Natural Heritage recently listed state areas that he considers excellent for bird watching. Included were Apple River Canyon, near Warren; Ferne Clyffe, Goreville; Fort Kaskaskia, Chester; Giant City, Makanda; Goose Lake Prairie, Morris; Horseshoe Lake, Cairo; Illinois Beach, Zion; Mississippi Palisades, Savanna; Pere Marquette, Grafton; Union County, Reynoldsville.

Visitors can obtain a list of state recreation areas from the Illinois Department of Conservation, Springfield.

Indiana

Although Indiana lacks the wide variety of habitat that might give it an abundance of species, it does have some choice bird-watching locations. The northern two thirds of the state is flat corn and hog country, where the once-abundant marshlands have long since been drained. The southern one third of the state is more rugged, and here the visitor travels through scenic wooded hill country.

Perhaps the best-known bird-watching extravaganza in Indiana comes in fall when the sandhill cranes are moving south. They may be seen for weeks, sometimes performing their courtship dances, in the Jasper-Pulaski Fish and Wildlife Area near Medaryville. There are few more spectacular birds anywhere. This is also a good area for waterfowl.

Another area worthy of note is the Indiana Dunes and Lake Michigan shoreline, especially during May when the spring migration is underway. Two state Fish and Wildlife Areas popular with birders in northern Indiana are Willow Slough and Jasper-Pulaski.

In the central part of the state there is the Atterbury Fish and Wildlife Area as well as Eagle Creek Park at Indianapolis, and the Brookville Reservoir. Near Seymour is Muscatatuck National Wildlife Refuge, which attracts visiting birders from considerable distance to see ducks, geese, and others. Photo blinds are provided. Best seasons are spring and fall.

Southern Indiana birders favor Monroe Reservoir in the Hoosier National Forest, Gibson Lake, and Minnehaha Fish and Wildlife Area as well as Harrison-Crawford State Forest.

Iowa

Perhaps the greatest annual event in the world of birds within the state of Iowa is the spring arrival of thousands of snow and blue geese, which reach the state in the last half of March. For those who happen to be in the southwestern part of Iowa then, a visit to Forney Lake and the Riverton area in Fremont County will be productive. This is another of those states where uniformity of terrain and vegetation makes for a limited variety of bird species. Most of the marshes that once drew birds here by the millions have long since been drained. In one area, Union Slough National Wildlife Refuge, the marshes have been restored, however, and here one may encounter breeding waterfowl as well as marsh birds in considerable variety. This refuge is near Algona. It is especially attractive during spring and fall migrations.

There are two other national wildlife refuges that anyone searching for birds in Iowa should know. One is the Mark Twain National Wildlife Refuge on the Mississippi River in the southeastern part of the state. The headquarters is at Quincy. The other is De Soto National Wildlife Refuge at Missouri Valley.

Near Ottumwa, six miles west of Drakesville, is Lake Wapello State Park. During migrations you may encounter Canada geese, snow geese, white pelicans, and other waterfowl in some variety here.

Would you like to see a hundred or more bald eagles at one time? Thousands of people have this experience every year during the Bald Eagle Appreciation Days when eagles are concentrated along the Mississippi River for the winter. Several hundred bald eagles winter in the Keokuk area in the southeastern corner of the state. Eagles also concentrate at Red Rock Reservoir.

Another giant bird showing up in Iowa each year is the American white pelican. The pelicans come to Red Rock and a few other good feeding areas from late August through late September.

Another area offering wide variety in bird species lies in the northwestern part of the state, in that region of lakes around the town of Spirit Lake. This is especially good territory for migrating waterfowl, spring and fall.

Kansas

Most people who know the birds of Kansas agree that the state's top birding area is Cheyenne Bottoms Waterfowl Management Area, covering 19,000 acres six miles northeast of Great Bend. Waterfowl descend on these wetlands by the hundreds of thousands, making it one of the most important fall migration stops in the Central Flyway. There are also thousands of migrant shorebirds to be seen here in both spring and fall. Bald eagles come to winter and roost in a large grove of cottonwoods near the marsh. The bird list, compiled by Kansas Department of Wildlife and Parks, totals some 320 species.

Another waterfowl management area maintained by the state is Marais des Cygnes near Pleasanton. The 6,563 acres, with 1,800 acres of water, attracts some 70,000 ducks, which spend the entire winter. Here you are likely to encounter blue-winged teal, pintails, mallards, shovelers, widgeon, scaup, and gadwall, along with egrets, herons and. shorebirds of wide variety.

Neosho Waterfowl Management Area, one mile east of St. Paul, has a variety of habitat that is attractive to birds.

Near Kirwin is the Kirwin National Wildlife Refuge, where more than 10,000 acres of wildlife lands attract sandhill cranes, shorebirds, ducks, geese, and thousands of other birds during their migration. There are also good wintering populations of waterfowl on this refuge. The refuge bird list contains 179 species.

Also productive, especially for prairie species, is Cimarron National Grassland, near Elkhart, in the southwestern corner of Kansas.

Another national wildlife refuge is Quivira, near Stafford. Check this one for the waterfowl, marsh birds, and species normally found in the open range lands and farm lands. It is excellent birding territory, with a bird list totaling 270 species.

Southeast of Emporia near Hartford is the Flint Hills National Wildlife Refuge, highly recommended by local birders.

Kentucky

Kentucky has an abundance of excellent areas for bird watching. Mammoth Cave National Park, near Cave City, is famed for its underground attraction but has more than fifty thousand acres of fine woodlands, with a variety of native birds for those who search them out.

Perhaps the most famous of all Kentucky bird watching spots is the Falls of the Ohio right in the city of Louisville. The Bernheim Forest, south of Louisville, is also excellent for birding.

The white-breasted nuthatch is skilled at climbing either up or down the trunks of trees in search of hidden insects.

John James Audubon knew of the riches of this area and wrote about the birds he saw there. Another area connected with Audubon is the Audubon State Park, near Henderson. Audubon was a resident of this part of Kentucky, and while a merchant there, painted the local birds. The museum has a fine collection of his works, including a complete set of the rare elephant folio. The park is especially good for forest-dwelling species.

In this western end of Kentucky, visitors often include the Ballard County Wildlife Management Area in their itinerary. It has a richness of bird life all year, including migratory shorebirds and wading birds. It is particularly noted for its Canada geese and other waterfowl in fall and winter. It is near La Center and Barlow. Another famous wildlife area in this region is the Reelfoot National Wildlife Refuge. (See Tennessee, page 185.)

Between the giant Kentucky and Barkley reservoirs lies the Land Between the Lakes National Recreation Area, an important wintering area for bald eagles. The visitor here also stands a chance of seeing wild turkeys.

The eastern part of Kentucky is mountain country, with its own species of wildlife. The Minor Clark Fish Hatchery at Moorhead attracts herons, gulls, shorebirds—and birders. Throughout the state are wildlife management areas often visited by local bird watchers. These areas, managed by the Department of Fish and Wildlife Resources, include Kleber, near Monterey, Henderson Sloughs, near Henderson, and the Lloyd area, not far from Crittenden.

Louisiana

Louisiana's extensive coastal marshes on the Gulf of Mexico form the southern terminus in the migratory travels of many North American birds, particularly ducks and geese. These coastal regions also are the launching areas from which southbound migrating land birds cross the Gulf of Mexico for Central and South America. The largest river-basin swamp in the United States, the Atchafalaya, lies between Baton Rouge and Lafayette.

Louisiana birders should investigate the following places of special interest. East of Shreveport, in the northwestern part of the state, is Lake Bistineau State Park, highly recommended by experienced Louisiana ornithologists. Another state park of special interest is Chicot, north of Ville Platte. Lacassine National Wildlife Refuge is near Lake Arthur. Sabine National Wildlife Refuge, in the very southwestern corner of the state, has a bird list with 242 species and in winter may host Canada, white-fronted, and blue and snow geese by the thousands. Blues and snows are often seen feeding in the marshes from Highway 27, the only road through this sprawling 142,000-acre refuge.

Nearby on Highway 82 is Cameron, another bird-watching area, famous among the members of the Orleans Audubon Society. Members of that group recommend Hackberry Woods, East Jetty, East Jetty Woods, Cameron Prairie, Backridge, and Magnolia Road, at the southern boundary of Sabine. West of Cameron on Highway 82 is the Holleyman-Sheely Migratory Bird Sanctuary maintained by the Baton Rouge Audubon Society. This is an especially good birding area during migrations.

The state's big Rockefeller Refuge can then be reached by traveling east from Cameron on 82. This is a wildlife wonderland, with large numbers of alligators, including some giants by today's standards, and an abundance of birds, particularly the wintering waterfowl for which this refuge is a prime attraction. In winter, the ducks and geese here may number 600,000 birds. The rice and crawfish farming areas of southwestern Louisiana are excellent possibilities for finding shorebirds as well as geese, ducks, wading birds, and rails.

Avery Island, southwest of New Iberia, offers special provisions and attractions for visiting bird watchers. Admission is charged to this outstanding sanctuary.

Grand Isle, about a hundred highway miles south of New Orleans, is particularly favored by Orleans Audubon Society members, who come to list reddish egrets, terns, knots, ruddy turnstones, clapper rails, frigatebirds, and others, especially wetland species.

Maine

Near Calais, in Maine, is the 22,565-acre Moosehorn National Wildlife Refuge. Bird watchers have listed 218 species here. Excellent trails and roads lead to the refuge's pine, spruce, and hardwood forests and the lakes, streams, and marshes hidden in them. This refuge is especially well known for its woodcock, black ducks, and ring-necked ducks. On a late evening between April 20 and May 10, you may witness the spectacular courting performance of the woodcock. Petit Manan NWR, near Milbridge, has some 280 recorded species, including many marine birds.

Perhaps the best known of Maine's state parks is Baxter, an extensive wilderness area that includes Mount Katahdin (elevation 5,267 feet) and where the forests are interspersed with lakes and streams. This is considered excellent hiking country and consequently should be of special interest to outdoorsmen who enjoy backpacking trips. Forest-dwelling species, including kinglets, warblers, crossbills, and woodpeckers, are prominent.

Visitors to Acadia National Park in Bar Harbor should stop at park headquarters for information on the birds of that area. This is a particularly good area for northern forest birds, and one may find a variety of warblers, flycatchers, white-throated sparrows, hermit and Swainson's thrushes, and golden-crowned kinglets. Boat trips available in this area bring birders close to marine birds—even whales. The ferry from Bar Harbor to Halifax, Nova Scotia, adds the possibility of listing shearwaters, fulmars, petrels, and other pelagic species.

Reid State Park can be reached out of Woolwich. Here one finds several habitat types, including rocky coast, salt marsh, sandy beaches, and coniferous forests. A number of land birds including red-breasted nuthatches and pileated woodpeckers are good possibilities. Summer visitors should scan offshore waters for sea ducks and gannets and also should look for shorebirds.

Other favorite bird-finding areas among citizens of Portland and surrounding towns are the Scarboro salt marshes and the Prouts Neck region. Here one may encounter a variety of shorebirds as well as gulls, loons, and ducks. In the Portland area, during the spring migration in May, there are excellent populations of warblers in Baxter's Woods near the Evergreen Cemetery, which itself is good birding territory.

Those who can make arrangements with boat captains may have unusual experiences visiting offshore islands along the Maine coast. Particularly well known for its birds is Machias Seal Islands, where puffins nest during the summer months.

At Falmouth, near Portland, a stop at the headquarters of Maine Audubon Society can be rewarding. Ask for a copy of the Society folder on its "Wildlife Sanctuaries and Nature Centers." These areas, including coastal headlands, lakeshores, estuaries, islands, and inland forests, are open free of charge, dawn to dusk, the year around. The folder gives details on nine of the most popular birding areas managed by the Society. "The Store" at the Society headquarters carries a wide selection of natural history books.

Maryland

Among the choice bird-watching areas in Maryland is the 14,263-acre Blackwater National Wildlife Refuge near Cambridge. Birders have recorded 231 species here and come to the refuge in winter months, especially for a view of the thousands of Canada geese that arrive to spend the winter. They may also see snow geese and many kinds of ducks.

Waterfowl and shorebirds by the thousands migrate along Maryland's shoreline, particularly in October and November. Assateague Island, a barrier island along the Atlantic Ocean, is especially productive in the fall. There are shorebirds on the mudflats, wading birds in the marshes, and occasionally peregrine falcons in the air. The returning birds can be seen again during the spring migrations in March and April. Concentrations of land birds also navigate along the shores and barrier beaches, with fall migrations usually well under way in September.

The mountains of western Maryland are excellent for breeding warblers and other forest birds.

Massachusetts

This state's, productive birding areas are numerous and well known. The Massachusetts Audubon Society maintains in excess of eighty sanctuaries totaling some 21,000 acres. Eighteen of these areas are permanently staffed. They are widely scattered across Massachusetts, so that no matter where you are in the Bay State you cannot be far from an Audubon sanctuary. For details and up-to-the-minute information on these areas, as well as bird watching in Massachusetts in general, write the Massachusetts Audubon Society, Lincoln, Mass. 01773. The organization publishes a *Birder's Kit* containing a variety of materials of interest to bird watchers.

Well known to Massachusetts birders is Plum Island, in the far northeastern corner of the state between the mouths of the Merrimac and Ipswich rivers. Much of this island lies within the Parker River National Wildlife Refuge. Bird watchers may see purple sandpipers, horned larks, Lapland longspurs, snow buntings, and Ipswich sparrows. There may be horned grebes, king eiders, oldsquaw, and even Harlequin

ducks. kittiwakes, murres, dovekies, and other alcids may be spotted by fortunate bird watchers in late fall or winter.

At the elbow of Cape Cod is Monomoy National Wildlife Refuge, an important area for black ducks, eiders, scoters, and shorebirds. This refuge can be reached by boat out of Chatham, but these waters are hazardous and the trip should not be attempted by anyone not familiar with the area. The safest plan is to arrange a trip with a local expert boatman or an organized Audubon birding event.

Michigan

Every part of Michigan has excellent birding areas. Among the better known in the upper peninsula is the Seney National Wildlife Refuge, established by the federal government in 1935 primarily for waterfowl. Canada geese now nest in this open marsh country, where they did not nest prior to establishment of the refuge. These resident geese, acting as decoys, draw in thousands of wild migrating geese during the autumn months, and with them may come snow geese and blue geese. The Michigan Department of Natural Resources has also released trumpeter swans in its effort to restore this giant bird to the state. A variety of ducks also nest here and visit the refuge during migration. The bird list for the refuge totals more than two hundred species. The refuge can be reached from Highway 77, two miles north of Germfask. In addition to its waterfowl, this refuge boasts breeding populations of sandhill cranes, yellow rails, and Le Conte's sparrows.

While in the upper peninsula, if you care to search for northern breeding species, proceed by Highway 77 to the Schoolcraft-Alger County line, because in this vicinity birders have been recording nesting pairs of yellow-bellied flycatchers, parula warblers, Lincoln's sparrows, and black-capped chickadees.

The endangered Kirtland's warbler nests on the ground beneath small jack pines in the Huron National Forest in northern Michigan. *Dow Chemical Company.*

Six miles south of the city of Saginaw, birders can turn off to the headquarters of Shiawassee National Wildlife Refuge, an area of 8,850 acres where more than 187 species of birds have been recorded. Birds found here will vary from season to season, with spring and fall bringing excellent concentrations of ducks, geese, swans, and other migrants.

The Michigan Department of Natural Resources maintains, on Saginaw Bay near Bay City, an unusual wildlife area known as Tobico Marsh. Here bird watchers turn their binoculars on numerous species of waterfowl and marsh birds during both the nesting seasons and the migratory periods of the year.

Other excellent bird-watching locations abound in Michigan. Most of the state parks and game areas are good birding territory at

A National Forest Service sign in Michigan tells the strange story of the rare Kirtland's warbler. Visiting birders can join tour groups to see this warbler on its nesting grounds.

some season. Lists of these can be obtained from the Michigan Department of Natural Resources, Box 30028, Lansing, Mich. 48909. Also helpful is the Michigan Audubon Society's booklet *Enjoying Birds in Michigan*.

Minnesota

The Minnesota Department of Natural Resources maintains numerous wildlife management areas, and although purchased with hunting license funds, these provide bird-watching opportunities. Two considered excellent for the bird watcher are Lac qui Parle, near Appleton, and Thief Lake, near Gatzke. Agassiz National Wildlife Refuge, also in this area out of Thief River Falls, has large populations of nesting waterfowl, gulls, cormorants, and other wetland species.

Duluth is a famous area for viewing migrating hawks in early autumn. The third week of September is usually best, and people with binoculars concentrate on the hill along Skyline Parkway above the city.

There are many excellent places to watch waterfowl during the fall and early winter migrations, but do not overlook the marshes near the town of Weaver in the Upper Mississippi National Wildlife and Fish Refuge. Other national wildlife refuges that provide Minnesota birders with excellent opportunities are Sherburne, Tamarac, and Rice Lake. Check also the Swan Lake area northwest of Mankato and the Minnesota River Valley between Shakopee and Mankato. East of Hinckley is St. Croix State Park, well known to Minnesota bird watchers.

Mississippi

Winter is a particularly interesting season in Mississippi, with the large numbers of migrants that have come South for the cold months. Check the coastal areas in and around Gulfport and Biloxi for waterfowl, loons, grebes, cormorants, plovers, turnstones, and numerous other shorebirds.

In winter, large concentrations of waterfowl can be seen at Yazoo and Noxubee National Wildlife Refuges, as well as Sardis Waterfowl Refuge, which supports a wintering flock of several thousand giant Canada geese. Noxubee National Wildlife Refuge near Brooksville covers 44,800 acres and also has wild turkeys. Of interest, offshore in Louisiana waters, is the Gulf Islands National Wildlife Refuge, with its nesting concentrations of shorebirds and water birds. Gulf Islands National Seashore is still another popular birding area in this region. Search the beaches, marshes, and savannas for their great variety of bird life. The Mississippi sandhill crane is a year-round resident of Jackson County.

Reservoirs in north and central Mississippi usually have a few bald eagles during the winter months. Mississippi has a number of colonies of the rare red-cockaded woodpecker along the Natchez Trace Parkway and on Noxubee National Wildlife Refuge, as well as in some of the national forest areas in the state.

Missouri

The variety of habitat types in Missouri, ranging from the prairie through the Ozarks to the Mississippi River lowlands, helps to account for Missouri's bird list of almost four hundred species. In autumn, waterfowl, shorebirds, and other wetland species move down the valley of the Mississippi and are seen on the mud bars, lakes, ponds, and sloughs throughout the state in the eastern part of the state. In winter the St. Louis segment of the Mississippi River can be excellent for gulls. Nearly one-third of the world's species of gulls have been recorded here.

Swan Lake National Wildlife Refuge, in the north-central part of the state, near Sumner, is river-bottom land where large concentrations of waterfowl winter.

The Springdale Bird Sanctuary maintained by the Audubon Society of Missouri is near Cape Girardeau. Visiting birders are welcome here. Columbia birders are partial to the East Ashland Conservation Area. Another excellent area for shorebirds, waterfowl, and other wetland species is the Squaw Creek National Wildlife Refuge, north of St. Joseph, near Mound City.

Experienced Missouri bird watchers also recommend a number of the state's wildlife management areas, including Duck Creek and adjacent Mingo National Wildlife Refuge, near Puxico, and Taborville Prairie, near Appleton City. A list of these public areas can be obtained from the Missouri Department of Conservation, P.O. Box 180, Jefferson City, Mo. 65102-0180.

Montana

Montana is big country, with a bird list totaling 345 species. One of my favorite Montana birding places is the famed Red Rock Lakes National Wildlife Refuge in the Centennial Valley, reached either from Monida or out of West Yellowstone. It was on this refuge that federal government biologists rescued the trumpeter swan, the world's largest waterfowl, from extinction in the Lower 48 states. The giant swans are seen there the year around, either as they ride on the shallow ponds or fly over the valley, filling the mountain air with their deep-throated calls. Here also are nesting sandhill cranes and a variety of other birds. This is remote, unforgettable country, but, because of the severe winters, go only in summertime.

Another top bird-watching location in Montana is Flathead Lake, south of Kalispell. Watch here for osprey nests.

Canyon Ferry Reservoir, between Helena and Townsend in the western part of the state, also has ospreys, as well as pelicans, cormorants, waterfowl, and a variety of marsh birds. November and December bring a concentration of bald eagles to Hauser Lake below Canyon Ferry Dam.

Glacier National Park has a limited number of species. Ask the park naturalist for the best current suggestions. Ptarmigan live here.

Bowdoin Lake National Wildlife Refuge, in the prairie country of north-central Montana, north of Malta, is an excellent summer birding area. Canada geese, great blue herons, cormorants, gulls, pelicans, ducks, and shorebirds nest here.

Still other top birding spots in Montana include Freezeout Lake, near Fairfield, Benton Lake National Wildlife Refuge, northwest of Great Falls, Charles M. Russell National Wildlife Range, adjacent to Fort Peck Reservoir, National Bison Range, out of Dixon, Lee Metcalf National Wildlife Refuge, near Stevensville, and the fish hatchery at Miles City.

Nebraska

In the panhandle area of western Nebraska, twenty-eight miles north of Oshkosh, lies the 46,000-acre Crescent Lake National Wildlife Refuge. The major attractions are waterfowl, shorebirds, and songbirds. There is also the possibility of seeing prairie chickens and long-billed curlews. More than 218 species of birds have been recorded on this refuge.

Another important national wildlife refuge is Fort Niobrara and the adjoining Niobrara River near Valentine. The government maintains a herd of old-fashioned Texas longhorn cattle on this refuge. Also in this sandhill section of the state is the Valentine National Wildlife Refuge, covering more than 71,000 acres and serving as the home of ducks, geese, sharp-tailed grouse, and a profusion of shorebirds. There is a good opportunity here to see pronghorn antelope as well. Throughout this famed sandhill region there is an abundance of lakes and marshes and always the possibility of encountering waterfowl and interesting shorebirds. In spring, there is a good chance of seeing the courting prairie chickens on their booming grounds. To make viewing of this prairie grouse spectacular easier, there are observation and photo blinds for public use at the Burchard Lake Wildlife Management Area in Pawnee County and in the Halsey National Forest.

The Platte River Valley, during migrations, draws large numbers of birds, including remarkable populations of ducks and geese. In the Lake McConaughy and Kearney areas, there is an excellent possibility of viewing wintering bald eagles. From Kearney to Grand Island is the spring staging grounds for large numbers of sandhill cranes.

A number of other highly productive bird-watching spots that should not be overlooked in Nebraska are Plattsmouth State Waterfowl Refuge, near Plattsmouth, De Soto National Wildlife Refuge, near Blair, Rainwater Basin area in Clay County, Halsey National Forest, near Halsey, and Oglala National Grasslands, in the northwestern corner of the state.

Nevada

Nevada has a remarkable variety of birds, thanks in part to the range in elevations from 500 feet to more than 13,000 feet above sea level, which accounts for a diversity of habitats. A Nevada Department of Wildlife non-game biologist says, "We have about 350 species of non-game birds, 22 species of waterfowl, and 12 species of upland-game birds." The deserts, the central mountain ranges, and the northeastern section of the state all offer interesting birding. Any source of water, flowing or still, should be investigated. One such area is the Stillwater Wildlife Management Area at Fallon, which has nesting populations of redhead ducks, mallards, teal, pintails, gadwalls, Canada geese, and coots. White-faced ibis and white pelicans are listed here. Spring and fall migrations bring other species through this area. Local bird watchers also point to the nearby Lahontan Valley and its

lakes, where a wide variety of interesting birds has been listed.

Out of Las Vegas the Desert National Wildlife Range provides some interesting bird-watching opportunities, especially around the refuge headquarters, which is an oasis.

The coniferous stands in the national forest lands around Lake Tahoe are excellent hunting grounds for nesting forest species, which might add new birds to the life lists of visiting naturalists from other parts of the country. Look for various species of thrushes, warblers, vireos, and woodpeckers.

Wildlife management areas maintained by the Department of Fish and Game also offer good opportunities for finding birds, including shorebirds and marsh-dwelling species. These state areas can be located through the Department of Fish and Game in Reno, or by inquiring locally in towns visited.

New Hampshire

From sea level to Mount Washington's peak, New Hampshire bird watchers encounter a wide variety in habitat and bird species. The Audubon Society of New Hampshire suggests a number of the state's top bird-watching areas, starting in the south and going northward. During migrations Hampton-Seabrook Harbor and Estuary can provide a highly productive day of viewing gulls, terns, and shorebirds. Great Bay is excellent for migratory and wintering waterfowl. Pow Wow Pond, at Kingston, is also rated high for viewing migrating waterfowl.

Near Chesterfield is Spofford Lake, and at Hinsdale is Lake Wantastiquet, both excellent locations for studying migratory waterfowl and other water birds.

In the south-central part of New Hampshire, Turkey Pond at Concord and the Merrimack River Valley between Concord and Boscawen are year-round favorites for both water birds and land species.

The Laconia area, in the central part of the state, is also good for both land and water species all year.

In the White Mountains of the northern part of New Hampshire, bird watchers find northern land species, some as summer residents, others throughout the year.

The Littleton area can be productive the year around for both water and land species.

Pontook Reservoir, north of Milan, offers both migratory waterfowl and others that stay for the summer nesting season.

Errol and Lake Umbagog are known to New Hampshire birders for their northern migratory species and a mixture of year-round land and water birds.

Of the wildlife management areas maintained by the New Hampshire Fish and Game Department, two come widely recommended. One is Adams Point on Great Bay in the town of Durham. The other is Wilder Waterfowl Management Area, on the Connecticut River in Lyme, where, in seasons of migration, a variety of species can be observed along the Connecticut River.

New Jersey

Among the more remarkable sights a bird watcher can witness is the concentration of brant that descend in autumn on the Edwin B. Forsythe, formerly Brigantine, National Wildlife Refuge, near Atlantic City, New Jersey. They come out of the distant north and descend in the night by the thousands on the refuge impoundments. The next morning the dark little geese ride in tight formations, feeding on the aquatic plants that grow there in abundance. This is the most important single wintering area known to the brant. In addition, the refuge appeals to a wide range of other species. Its 13,442 acres of salt marsh and sandhills is one of the most popular birding areas in the East. It draws thousands of bird watchers annually. Many come from Philadelphia, scarcely

sixty miles away, or New York City, a little more than one hundred miles to the north. Refuge headquarters offers a free bird list.

Cape May is another notable location that has attracted New Jersey bird watchers for decades. At Cape May Point State Park and the nearby Cape May Bird Observatory, a parade of migrants, sometimes in great numbers, passes through in late summer and fall.

In the northern part of New Jersey is a large marsh and swamp known as Troy Meadows, a noted wetland bird-watching area almost in the shadow of Manhattan. Spring and fall migrations bring ducks, rails, and other wetland species to Troy Meadows. The area is northeast of Morristown. Among the best spots is Higbee Beach Wildlife Management Area, the Great Swamp National Wildlife Refuge west of Newark near Basking Ridge, and Island Beach State Park, a barrier island along Barnegat Bay.

New Mexico

New Mexico has a wide variety of life zones and habitat types and is often a meeting ground for northern and southern species. One of the state's leading authorities on finding New Mexico birds tells us that the following are considered among the very best areas by that state's resident bird watchers.

The Rio Grande in the Los Alamos area is excellent. In particular, check Gutierrez Park and the ponds near Espanola, twenty-five miles north of Santa Fe. Then west of San Juan Pueblo, a few miles north of Espanola, both sides of the Rio Grande are good. In fact, almost any place along the Rio Grande is considered excellent birding. In this same area there is good bird watching in the Santa Cruz, Cundiyo, and Tesuque areas.

When you are in the Albuquerque area, check north of town in the foothills of the Rio Grande near Alameda Town.

Another area particularly promising for bird

watchers is in the Las Vegas National Wildlife Refuge near Las Vegas, New Mexico.

Then, near the Colorado line in the Chama area, is the Los Ojos Fish Hatchery, which on the maps is marked Park View. In addition, this area also offers excellent birding through the Brazos Canyon and around Burford and Hopewell lakes. These areas are all within a few miles south of Chama.

In the southwestern part of the state lies Silver City, and west of it, between Red Rock and Cliff, the Gila River is considered one of the best of all New Mexican regions for those trying to compile a large bird list. If you are traveling in a four-wheel-drive vehicle, do not overlook remote campgrounds such as Willow Springs and others in the Gila National Forest. For birders these areas are considered well worth the trouble needed to reach them. Southwest of Animas is Guadalupe Canyon, used by many Mexican bird species as a flyway route.

Near Maxwell, the Maxwell National Wildlife Refuge has several lakes that are a great attraction for waterfowl, shorebirds, and other wetland species. Another national wildlife refuge is Bosque del Apache, south of San Antonio. Near Roswell is the Bitter Lake National Wildlife Refuge, also considered excellent by resident birders. Do not overlook the Bandelier National Monument northwest of Santa Fe.

In the eastern part of the state, south of Portales, between Dora and Milnesand, the lesser prairie chickens engage in their courtship dances in early April. Those interested should first inquire of the New Mexico Game and Fish Department at Santa Fe.

New York
Ranging from the Lake Erie shores, through New York's forests and mountains, to the Atlantic is a variety of bird-watching areas greater than we can do justice to in this limited space. But determined birders can discover other areas by consulting with local bird watchers and park naturalists. In the Finger Lakes Region, you can visit Montezuma National Wildlife Refuge, northeast of Seneca Falls. This refuge, covering 6,400 acres, was set aside primarily for ducks and geese, but in its open marsh, swamp, and woodlands, birders have found more than 250 species. Among them are mallards, wood ducks, black ducks, gadwalls, shovelers, redheads, and ruddy ducks. The best times at Montezuma for migrating waterfowl come in early April and late October.

Two other national wildlife refuges of importance to birders are Morton, at Sag Harbor, and Iroquois, at Basom, which is a particularly good area for observing waterfowl during spring migration.

Near Ithaca, the home of Cornell University, the better bird-watching places include Taughannock Falls State Park, north of the city on the west shore of Lake Cayuga. The spectacular gorge cutting through this state park has climatic conditions that attract species of birds that more commonly nest far to the north. Also in this area is the famous Sapsucker Woods, the research area maintained by the Cornell University Laboratory of Ornithology.

Well known to New York birders is Montauk Point, at the eastern end of Long Island, reached from the village of Montauk and a particularly rich area for winter bird watching.

North Carolina
One of the most popular areas in North Carolina for bird watching is along the Outer Banks, that ribbon of sand that buffers the mainland from the rough waters of the Atlantic. A large part of this area is in federal ownership. Here are found the Pea Island National Wildlife Refuge, the Cape Hatteras National Seashore, and Cape Lookout National Seashore managed by the National Park Service. Also on this eastern side of the state are Roanoke River, Alligator

River and Pocosin Lakes National Wildlife Refuges, all excellent birding areas. Migrating birds follow this shore line by the hundreds of thousands, while interesting summer residents come to these sandy places to nest. Here are found wading birds of many kinds—gulls, terns, gannets, and skimmers. Smaller songbirds also migrate along the Outer Banks.

Other national wildlife refuges in North Carolina include Mattamuskeet, Swan Quarter, and Pungo. All have concentrated populations of waterfowl and wading birds.

The Piedmont area, in the central part of the state, has less variety for bird watching than the extreme eastern or the western portions. Near Wadesboro is the Pee Dee National Wildlife Refuge. In the Great Smoky Mountains, both the National Park and the U.S. Forest Service lands offer opportunities for backpacking into remote areas. Also of interest are the Joyce Kilmer Memorial Forest and the TVA lakes, including Fontana, Nantahala, and Hiwassee. In the Great Smoky Mountains National Park, park naturalists conduct frequent special programs on the natural history of the area.

The Blue Ridge Parkway has many overlooks where people can park for bird watching.

North Dakota

Historically, the wetland prairies in North Dakota have attracted magnificent concentrations of shorebirds and waterfowl. Canada geese, snows, and blues flock down through the Dakota country during the migration seasons. So do sandhill cranes by the hundreds, while flocks of white pelicans pull themselves slowly across the open skies.

Because of its importance to waterfowl, this state has become a concentration center of national wildlife refuges. Among the better-known waterfowl refuges for both migrant and nesting birds are J. Clark Salyer National Wildlife Refuge, near Upham; Upper Souris, near Foxholm; Lostwood, near Lostwood; Arrowwood, near Kensal; Long Lake, at Moffit; and Des Lacs, at Kenmare. Chase Lake NWR, administered out of Arrowwood NWR, is a wilderness area where vehicles are forbidden. Living here are more than 10,000 white pelicans—the world's largest nesting colony—along with cormorants and thousands of gulls. Visitors may walk the refuge boundaries but are not permitted on the islands where the pelicans nest.

Ohio

Marblehead Peninsula is a long-time favorite with birders, especially in May during the spring migration. The Lake Erie marsh country in this northwestern corner of Ohio attracts large numbers of waterfowl, shorebirds, raptors, and others. Also, along this shore lies the state-owned Magee Marsh Wildlife Area and the adjoining Ottawa National Wildlife Refuge, both managed for waterfowl production. The Magee Marsh Wildlife Area's famous birding trail at Crane Creek State Park attracts thousands of people every year. You may see here more than twenty species of warblers during the spring migration.

In nearby Toledo the Woodland Cemetery is considered a top birding area, as is Maumee Bay on the east edge of the city. The Flats of the Maumee River are good for shorebirds from July through.

Grand Lake on the western side of Ohio is a favorite among area birders.

In the wooded hill country of southern Ohio there is extensive timberland mixed with farmland in Pike State Forest, Shawnee State Forest, and Wayne National Forest. Wild turkeys are again common through the hill country, and the gobblers are heard in spring and summer.

Other areas favored by Ohio birders include

Carolina wren, a common and popular resident of many backyards, arrives at its nest with a worm for its young. *Peter and Stephen Maslowski.*

Oklahoma

Habitat types in Oklahoma vary from the hills and forests in the eastern part through the high-grass prairies of the central portion of Oklahoma, with its wooded river bottoms, toward the mixed grass areas of the West. Consequently, this is a transition area, where eastern species begin to give way to those more commonly found in the West. This makes it an interesting and productive area for bird watchers in almost any season.

Birders here know of three major concentration areas where migrating egrets, herons, and other birds congregate. One is at Bethany, another near Muskogee, in the eastern part of Oklahoma, and the third near Haskell, just south of Tulsa.

The national wildlife refuges in Oklahoma provide excellent bird-watching areas, and perhaps the best known of all is Wichita Mountains near Cache. There is an excellent opportunity here to see wild turkeys as well as a number of other birds. In addition to the bird life, the elk, deer, bison, prairie dogs, and large herds of Texas longhorn cattle are usually close enough to the roads to permit visiting photographers to take pictures of them.

Salt Plains National Wildlife Refuge, near Enid, is used heavily by geese, ducks, and white pelicans. Geese by the thousands descend on this refuge in winter and fall during the migration, and as many as forty thousand may stay for the winter months. Mallards are the predominant duck, followed by pintails and green-winged teal. Franklin's gulls and shorebirds are prominent among the 250 species on the refuge bird list.

When you are near Tishomingo, pay a visit to the Tishomingo National Wildlife Refuge and look for ducks, geese, and shorebirds. This area is adjacent to Lake Texoma and has a bird list totaling more than 225 species.

If you are in Stillwater, visit the Lake Carl Blackwell area, which is administered by the

Greenlawn Cemetery in Columbus, various state wildlife areas including Spring Valley, Killdeer Plains, Killbuck, and Hebron State Fish Hatchery. Tar Hollow State Forest, the Ross-Pickway County Line Road area, and Lorain Harbor are also productive.

Top birding areas in the southwestern corner of the state include Spring Grove Cemetery in Cincinnati, the Cincinnati Nature Center east of the city, and the Oxbow area, a wetland at the confluence of the Ohio and Great Miami Rivers where many kinds of waterfowl, wading birds, and shorebirds stop to rest and feed during migrations.

Sixty miles upstream, and bordering the Ohio River, is Adams County where birders list such southern species as black vulture and chuck-will's-widow.

Oklahoma Agricultural and Mechanical College. This rich area covers 21,000 acres, embracing tall-grass prairies and a large lake.

Robbers Cave State Park is a sizable forest game preserve near Wilburton, a picturesque area with varied vegetation and an impressive list of birds both migrant and resident.

Oregon

From the verdant rain forests of the Pacific Coast through the mountain strongholds of the Douglas fir and eastward into Oregon's drier lands, this is an area so rich in its bird-watching opportunities that we can only touch lightly on its possibilities. One of the genuine bird-watching spectaculars I have witnessed on this continent is to be found during the autumn months on the Malheur National Wildlife Refuge, out of Burns, Oregon. Pintails, mallards, and other ducks descend on this refuge by the hundreds of thousands. Among them are sandhill cranes and white pelicans, along with many kinds of marsh birds and shorebirds. Trumpeter swans nest here. In all, more than 230 birds are on this refuge list. Another spectacular area is that complex of state and national refuges around Klamath Falls. In Summer Lake is the Summer Lake Wildlife Management Area rated very high by Oregon's birders for nesting species in summer as well as migrants in both spring and fall.

Migratory birds are abundant in season at Fort Steven at the mouth of the Columbia River and at Tillamook Bay, which is especially noted for its shorebirds.

There is good bird finding throughout the Willamette Valley and eastward into the coniferous forest.

From Hood River a scenic circular drive will lead summer visitors upward toward Mount Hood through a variety of habitat types into the territories of western forest species.

For a complete guide to this state's birds, check bookstores for *The Birder's Guide to Oregon,* published by the Portland Audubon Society.

Pennsylvania

In autumn, the hawks funnel down through eastern Pennsylvania by the hundreds. The hawks include, among others, red-tailed, sharp-shinned, and now and then a rare peregrine falcon or an eagle. They catch the updrafts formed as winds from the west hit Kittatinny Ridge. They ride these winds with minimum effort, soaring along the ridges on their way South. There are other places in the country to see hawk migrations, but perhaps none better known than Pennsylvania's Hawk Mountain Sanctuary. On this refuge, north of Hamburg, an average of 15,000 birds of prey are seen during the autumn migration.

Presque Isle State Park, at Erie, is a good location for shorebirds, waterfowl, and a variety of land birds. Another western Pennsylvania bird-watching area of note is the Pymatuning Reservoir. The state manages this area for Canada geese and other waterfowl, but visitors can also record an abundance of songbirds. More than 100 species of birds nest in the Pymatuning area, including grebes, bitterns, rails, raptors, shorebirds, and smaller land birds.

In northeastern Pennsylvania the Pocono Mountains offer a diverse habitat rich in wildlife, especially forest-dwelling birds.

Birders in the Philadelphia area visit the Tinicum National Environmental Center to check for egrets, herons, and shorebirds as well as songbirds.

Rhode Island

"Without question," says a professional biologist employed by the state of Rhode Island, "our top bird-watching area is Block Island." This seven-mile-long island, south across Block Island Sound, is known among bird watchers for both

The southern bald
eagle has gradually
increased in num-
bers in recent times.
Winter concentra-
tions of these giant
birds bring hundreds
of eagle watchers to
choice locations in
several states.

its concentrations of migrating birds and its wintering species. A remarkable variety of birds, ranging from warblers to waterfowl, can be observed here at various seasons. Transportation to Block Island is by auto ferry and air.

The state maintains a number of hunting and wildlife areas. Perhaps the best of these for bird watching is the Great Swamp Wildlife Area, in the southwestern part of Rhode Island.

South Carolina

From its 281 miles of sandy coastline, South Carolina stretches inland and upward to the peaks of the Blue Ridge Mountains and is a land so varied that it has a remarkable population of birds. Some of the earliest and most famous bird watchers in American history traveled and studied here. Some 375 species of birds have been recorded.

Among the state's national wildlife refuges of special interest to bird watchers is Cape Romain, a coastal refuge with headquarters at Awendaw. This 60,000-acre refuge attracts geese, ducks, wild turkeys, shorebirds, gulls, and terns, and it even boasts a few alligators. Another national wildlife refuge is Carolina Sandhills, near McBee, with wintering Canada geese and 16 species of ducks. This is another place where it is possible to see wild turkeys. Bird watchers on Carolina Sandhills have recorded 190 species of birds. In addition, there is Santee National Wildlife Refuge near Summerton, a sprawling 74,000-acre wildlife area. Thousands of ducks and geese congregate here for the winter months. The refuge bird list contains 208 species.

South of Georgetown, where the bridge and causeway lead across the Santee River Delta, bird watchers often stop to study wildlife through binoculars and spotting scopes. There may be egrets, ducks, anhingas, and others. The 25,000-acre Santee Coastal Reserve, two miles east of HY 17 on Secondary Road 857, has red-cockaded woodpeckers, Bachman's sparrows, painted buntings, and a long list of others.

South Dakota

"Sand Lake National Wildlife Refuge," says one biologist with South Dakota's Department of Game, Fish, and Parks, "with its spectacular goose concentrations is a must." April and October are considered outstanding times here, with April somewhat better because, in fall, hunting makes the birds wary. Refuge headquarters is at Columbia.

The James River in this Brown County area is an artery along which passerines migrate. In the winter months, local birders go afield to list snowy owls, northern shrikes, redpolls, snow buntings, Lapland longspurs, and other visitors.

In the heart of the pothole and lake region around Webster are many areas noted for their migrating songbirds, particularly warblers.

The Waubay National Wildlife Refuge provides nesting grounds for grebes and Canada geese and also attracts a wide variety of migrants to its lakes and woods.

Bitter Lake, south of this refuge, is known for its white pelicans and double-crested cormorants during the nesting season.

Another productive area is Oakwood Lakes State Park, northwest of Brookings. This is known among birders as one of the state's top warbler areas.

Include in your South Dakota bird-watching areas the Big Sioux River near Sioux Falls.

In the vicinity of Pierre, the state capital, remember that this Missouri River town is a melting pot for birds common in many parts of the country. The area offers an opportunity to see greater prairie chickens, piping plovers, eastern bluebirds, dickcissels, Lapland longspurs, black-headed grosbeaks, burrowing owls, and many more.

According to state wildlife biologists of the South Dakota Department of Game, Fish, and Parks, Martin, in the southwestern part of the state, is another area that birders should visit. There, the Lacreek National Wildlife Refuge now has a successful breeding colony of trumpeter swans.

For variety, do not overlook the Black Hills area, where you may find the white-winged junco as a year-round resident.

At Wind Cave National Park a ranger who leads birding tours helped us find a black-backed woodpecker, black-headed grosbeak, solitary vireo, Bullock's oriole and lark sparrow.

Buffalo, in the northwestern corner of the state, is a land of rocky outcroppings and buttes with nesting golden eagles and other birds of prey.

Tennessee

"With a state as diverse as Tennessee," explains one noted Tennessee naturalist, "it is very difficult to select the best birding areas." Considering just the city of Chattanooga alone, one encounters a wide range of habitats and consequently a wide variety of birds. If you are traveling in this state it is a good plan to obtain, from the Tennessee Wildlife Resources Agency, in Nashville, a list of its wildlife management areas. Because of the habitat management in these areas, they offer excellent opportunities for finding birds.

In northwest Tennessee is the famed Reelfoot Lake, created by the New Madrid earthquake in 1812. Good populations of waterfowl are found at Reelfoot. There are also rookeries where herons nest, and ospreys also nest around the lake.

Along the shores of the giant Kentucky Lake, and also Old Hickory Reservoir, there are several wildlife management areas known to local birders for their shorebirds and waterfowl.

Within the Cherokee National Forest, in eastern Tennessee, is the Cherokee Management Area, widely known among Tennessee bird watchers for its warbler and hawk migrations.

In the north-central part of the state is Cross Creeks National Wildlife Refuge. It is on Highway 49, southeast of Dover. It has ponds, marshes, and woodlands, and bird watchers visiting the area have found more than two hundred species of birds. This refuge is particularly good for wintertime bird watching because it lures thousands of ducks and geese. Frequently birders here see a bald eagle.

Knoxville, home of the University of Tennessee, has a number of areas well known to local bird watchers, including Powell Marsh near Powell Airport. From here it is an easy drive to the Great Smoky Mountains National Park, where the birds have been studied in detail over the years by park naturalists and others. (See page 150)

Texas

For bird watchers, Texas ranks right at the top. No other state offers visitors from other sections of the country a better chance to add new species to life lists. Among the national wildlife refuges well known to Texas birders is Santa Ana, west of Brownsville. Covering only 2,000 acres, this refuge has some species found nowhere else in the United States. On our latest stop at Santa Ana we took advantage of the naturalist guided tour on the comfortable tram that carries birders over the refuge trails. Green jays were abundant along with the great kiskadee, plain chachalaca, and others that people from north of the Lower Rio Grande Valley rarely see.

Also in this part of Texas is the Laguna Atascosa National Wildlife Refuge, out of San Benito, with a bird list of 317 species. It always ranks high on Christmas bird counts.

The Texas Gulf Coast has one of the most famous of all national wildlife refuges, Aransas, winter home of all the world's remaining wild whooping cranes and more than 350 other species.

Muleshoe National Wildlife Refuge, meanwhile, winters the country's largest concentration of sandhill cranes. This refuge is out of Muleshoe.

Also on the Rio Grande is the Bentsen/Rio Grande Valley State Park, five miles south of

Greater roadrunner, fast enough on its feet to catch lizards, is often seen in the deserts of the Southwest.

Mission, a 588-acre sanctuary known as one of the finest bird-watching areas in the country.

The sprawling Falcon Reservoir, straddling the international border, draws visitors, including bird watchers, to the Falcon State Recreation Park.

In the Texas hill country, about ten miles east of Johnson City, is the 4,800-acre Pedernales Falls State Park, also a gem for those who study birds. There are often unusual western species to be seen in McKittrick Canyon within Guadalupe Mountains National Park, administered out of Carlsbad, NM.

South of Amarillo, Palo Duro Canyon State Park, one of Texas' popular vacation areas, is good bird-finding territory the year round.

In southwest Texas, Big Bend National Park borders the Rio Grande for 107 miles, and a visit to this scenic park is worth the trip. There are canyon towhees, painted buntings, ravens, numerous species of hawks, and more. There are also jack rabbits, collared peccaries, a race of miniature whitetail deer, and once a bobcat dashed across the road in front of our car. River runners can arrange for rafting trips or rental canoes at Study Butte near the park's western entrance. This is desert country where hikers on the numerous trails wear sturdy shoes and carry water.

Utah

This western state of varied environments has a bird list of more than 375 species, and perhaps, as Utah birders believe, others not yet identified. From the low elevations in the Mohave Desert in the southwest corner of Utah to the state's highest peaks, rising to more than 13,000 feet in the Uinta Mountains of the northeast, birders can expect surprises. Any oasis in the desert, especially during migrations, tends to attract concentrations of birds.

Some of the best birding anywhere is found around the Great Salt Lake. Three areas known to local birders as being especially productive are Farmington Bay Waterfowl Management Area at the mouth of the Jordan River, Willard

Bay between Ogden and Brigham City, and Antelope Island, a state park, and the causeway linking it to the mainland.

But for many the first choice birding area, one with an international reputation, is the Bear River Migratory Bird Refuge lying west of Brigham City. This national wildlife refuge covers thousands of acres of ponds and marshes where the Bear River empties into Great Salt Lake. Migration seasons bring incredible numbers of birds to these wetlands, and sixty species are known to nest here.

If you visit this refuge, plan to drive the twelve-mile self-guided road. The refuge, including its twelve-mile drive, was closed for some years when Great Salt Lake rose and flooded the area. But the water receded and the drive was reopened in 1990. I remember it especially for the ravens nesting in the observation towers which have since been destroyed by the flood. There are also American avocets, white-faced ibises, western grebes, willets, gulls, terns, cormorants, and numerous others.

Vermont

The forested mountains and green valleys of Vermont provide unlimited opportunities for bird watchers who are willing to get out, leave the traveled highways, and explore. There are both deciduous and coniferous forests. A number of state-owned areas, which local bird watchers know well, include the Dead Creek Waterfowl Management Area, at Addison, Sandbar Wildlife Management Area, at Milton, and Victory Wildlife Management Area, at Victory.

The Missisquoi National Wildlife Refuge on Lake Champlain, near Swanton, has a good population of waterfowl from early spring until fall freeze-up. This is a river delta flood plain at the mouth of the Missisquoi River some forty miles north of Burlington. The bird list here includes 185 species. Other productive areas include Wenlock Wildlife Management area at Ferdinand, Groton State Forest at Groton, and Green Mountain National Forest, especially the wilderness areas.

The Connecticut River can provide rewarding birding in spring and fall. So can the Tinmouth Channel, Tinmouth. South Bay at Newport also comes recommended by Vermonters, as does the famed Long Trail, a hiking trail maintained by the Green Mountain Club at Waterbury. The trail extends for 260 miles largely through forested mountain wilderness.

Virginia

Back Bay National Wildlife Refuge, Virginia Beach, covers about 4,600 acres and is famous for its waterfowl and shorebirds. Peak migration periods are December and March. Marshlands, sand dunes, and open water cover about half of the refuge. The bird list for this refuge totals 250 species. You will see, in particular, snow geese, Canada geese, mallards, green-winged teal, American widgeon, scaup, canvasback, and tundra swans. Wintering species include common loons, gulls, cormorants, horned larks, and savannah sparrows.

Greater snow geese, brant, ducks, and shorebirds are also seen by bird watchers visiting Chincoteague National Wildlife Refuge. This refuge, typical of the barrier islands found along the Atlantic Coast, has beach and low dunes as well as broad salt marshes and freshwater pools.

Do not overlook Presquile National Wildlife Refuge, with its large numbers of wintering Canada geese and blue phase snow geese. This refuge is reached out of Hopewell. State wildlife areas of special interest include Mockhorn Island, 9,100 acres of wetlands, on the Atlantic side of the eastern shore, and Hog Island Refuge in Surry County.

In the timber-covered mountains out of Front Royal is Shenandoah National Park and the Skyline Drive. In these wooded lands, visitors sometimes see common ravens, grosbeaks, ruffed grouse, and a variety of thrushes and warblers. There are foot trails through the park, including a lengthy section of the Appalachian Trail. The park naturalist can supply added information on bird-watching opportunities.

Washington

Variety and sweeping grandeur, unforgettable landscapes, and seascapes make the state of Washington a favorite with travelers whatever their interest. But this variety of habitat also helps to account for the fact that Washington has one of the most spectacular bird lists of all the states.

Through the first half of summer, nesting species in Mount Rainier National Park have their territories established among spectacular wildflower gardens. Check with the park naturalist for information on birds in the park.

Two other national parks, North Cascades and Olympic, also rate high. Olympic National Park, with its rain forests, coastal beaches, and mountain peaks, has a wide variety of species

These birders are counting black brant and snow geese on the Willapa National Wildlife Refuge on Washington's Pacific Coast. *David B. Marshall, U.S. Fish and Wildlife Service.*

ranging from oystercatchers and puffins at sea level to blue grouse and common ravens in the high country.

Excellent for wintering black brant and other waterfowl is Willapa National Wildlife Refuge, out of Ilwaco. Another national wildlife refuge is McNary, out of Burbank, with 3,600 acres for wintering waterfowl.

Scattered over Washington are a number of recreation and wildlife management areas maintained by the Department of Wildlife and many of these are frequently visited by bird watchers because of the variety of wildlife they support. The following are of special interest: Gloyd Seeps, north of the town of Moses Lake, has golden eagles, white pelicans, magpies, and ravens. Oyhut, at the southern end of Ocean Shores Peninsula, boasts excellent populations of shorebirds. John's River, twelve miles southwest of Aberdeen, has many coastal birds. W. T. Wooten, thirteen miles southwest of Dayton, is excellent birding country. So is Asotin Creek, thirteen miles southwest of the town of Asotin.

Among the most productive of all Washington birding locations is Puget Sound, with its broken coastline and offshore islands. Beach Drive is a popular route. Puffins, auklets, gulls, cormorants, and terns are recorded in this part of the state.

West Virginia

The mountain state of West Virginia has more and better bird-watching opportunities than is generally realized outside its borders. A remarkably large portion of this state lies within the boundaries of the Monongahela National Forest, with headquarters at Elkins. Within this forest are a number of unusual areas, including Gaudineer Knob, Cheat Mountain, and Dolly Sods, considered excellent by local birders during the fall migration, especially for hawk watching.

Canaan Valley and Blackwater Falls are known for their birding.

On their courting grounds, male greater prairie chickens compete at dawn for the females' attention. The Wisconsin prairie, where these birds were photographed, is one of the limited areas where greater prairie chickens are still found.

Cheat Lake, near Morgantown, is especially good in spring and fall. Another good place for listing migrants in these seasons is McClintic Wildlife Station near Point Pleasant.

Migrating hawks in autumn attract birders to the Hanging Rock Migratory Raptor Observatory atop Peters Mountain within the borders of Jefferson National Forest in Monroe County.

West Virginia birders also recommend the Cranesville Swamp, north of Terra Alta, Greenland Gap, at Scherr, Kates Mountain, at White Sulphur Springs, Holly River State Park, near Hacker, and Tomlinson Run State Park, near Chester.

In addition, Oglebay Park, six miles from downtown Wheeling, is widely known among birders.

Then there is the spectacular New River Gorge, and if you are visiting this valley you will do well to pick up a copy of *A Guide to the Birds of the New River Gorge Area,* for sale in local nature shops.

Wisconsin

Wisconsin is another of those states so rich in wildlife that we can only hope to list here some of the outstanding areas. In the state parks, state forests, national wildlife refuges, and elsewhere, there are swamps, forests, lakes, rivers, and open farm lands. Buena Vista Marsh in Central Wisconsin is the home of a famous population of greater prairie chickens. Near Horicon is the state-owned Horicon Marsh Wildlife Area and the adjoining Horicon National Wildlife Refuge, covering together nearly 32,000 acres.

Weekend bird watchers sometimes create traffic jams during the peak autumn migration as they park along Highway 49 to see Canada geese by the thousands.

Another National Wildlife Refuge, Necedah, seven miles west of Necedah, boasts a bird list of more than two hundred species, including sandhill cranes and a wide variety of waterfowl.

Wisconsin stations naturalists in several of its larger state parks, including Devil's Lake, Peninsula, Terry Andrae, Governor Dodge, and Kettle Moraine State Forest.

Those searching for interesting birds should not overlook the Audubon Camp of Wisconsin, at Sarona, Schlitz-Audubon Nature Center, at Milwaukee, River Edge Nature Center, at Milwaukee. In the northern part of the state the Long Island-Chequamegan area is an important staging area for migrating shorebirds, while the Apostle Islands area is considered excellent for migrating hawks.

Meadow Valley Wildlife Area, on Highway 73 near Tomah, has abundant waterfowl as well as upland species, including wild turkeys.

The Yellowstone Wildlife Area, out of Blanchardville or Darlington in southern Wisconsin, while not outstanding, has a variety of wading birds, waterfowl, and shorebirds and is also known for its spring warbler migration. Other state wildlife areas with excellent birding possibilities include the George W. Mead Wildlife Area, near Marshfield, Grand River, southeast of Montello, French Creek, in the south-central part of the state near Portage, Vernon Marsh, at Mukwonago, and the Van Loon Wildlife Area, twelve miles north of La Crosse. At Crek Meadows Wildlife Area in northwestern Wisconsin the Department of Natural Resources has reintroduced the trumpeter swan and there are several free flying breeding pairs in that part of the state.

Wyoming

In recent years, Soda Lake created near Casper by the American Oil Company as a waste pond has developed into a choice bird-watching area for Wyoming birders. Waterfowl stop here during migration, and some remain to nest. There are longspurs, hawks, and occasionally short-eared owls. Reports one Audubon Society member, "It is one of the finest observation places in the state."

The Yellowstone and Grand Tetons national parks are, of course, excellent birding territory. (See page 146) The National Elk Refuge, at Jackson has trumpeter swans as well as a number of species of ducks.

If you drive the highway between Cheyenne and Laramie, you can visit Pole Mountain within Medicine Bow National Forest. The wooded canyons, particularly the Vedauwoo Glen offer unusual birding opportunities in summer and fall.

The Ocean Lake Wildlife Management Area northwest of Riverton has a combination of marsh and shallow lake habitat that attracts shorebirds and other wetland species.

The Sheridan area, with vegetation ranging from grasslands to forested mountains, offers a good variety of birds. Lake DeSmit in this region is considered especially good birding.

There is also a wide diversity of bird life in the Black Hills and the Devils Tower area.

The Green River below Fontenelle Reservoir is considered especially productive for its spring warbler migrations.

More on Finding Birds

Beginning birders usually learn first to identify the birds coming to their yards. But a growing interest soon sends them searching out strange new birds in nearby areas. Every city has its choice birding locations—local parks and woodlands, open fields, ponds and marshes, and other habitat types. There may be nature centers, lakes, harbors, and wetlands that attract waterfowl shorebirds, wading birds, gulls, and various smaller birds. Do not overlook the cemeteries where mature trees attract warblers, orioles, tanagers, and other colorful birds, especially during migrations.

Local naturalists and members of bird clubs are usually generous in sharing information on where the good birding spots are. The city or county park districts, as well as the local nature center, natural history museum, or college or university department of zoology are good sources of leads on choice birding locations. So are the wildlife professionals working for the state conservation agency, which is probably listed in the capitol city's telephone directory. County conservation officers can direct inquiries to the appropriate office in their organization. Most states now have a "watchable wildlife" program that offers literature helpful to birders. The watchable wildlife program is part of a nationwide plan to create and preserve habitat and wildlife by stimulating interest in wildlife conservation.

Clear-cutting our mature forests has eliminated whole ecosystems with their forest birds. This trail in Okefenokee National Wildlife Refuge in Georgia is one of the remaining locations where birders find the rare red-cockaded woodpecker.

In many cities across America, birders can call special "bird alert" numbers and listen to a recorded message, revised weekly, telling where unusual and interesting birds are being seen currently. Tracking these local bird alert services down can be worth the effort for those wanting to add new species to their list. Serious birders traveling in strange cities find telephone numbers for bird alerts by calling the local Audubon Society chapter or bird club. Top birders in any community will know if the service exists and how to reach it. Knowledgeable birders can be found through birding supply stores, park district offices, nature centers, colleges, and natural history museums.

Birds and the Law

One of my neighbors has a special fondness for owls, and when he found a dead barred owl beside the highway one day, he came asking where he might get it mounted. "I'd just like to have it," he explained. I had to tell him that what he wanted to do is against the law—federal law—which prohibits the taking of or possession of, dead or alive, nearly all the wild birds, including birds of prey. He called the local conservation officer, who suggested that he donate the owl to the nearby museum of natural history, which could legally add it to its scientific collection, and that is where the barred owl that became a highway victim lies in state today.

There is sound reason for laws against the possession of wild birds. Such laws discourage those who might be tempted to take a live bird, then claim that it suffered an accidental death.

All native migratory birds occurring in the United States are protected by federal laws and international treaties. The exceptions are house sparrows, barnyard pigeons and starlings, but even these species are sometimes covered by state or municipal regulations that make killing them illegal.

There are legal hunting seasons during which game birds may be taken within a framework of laws. States set these laws for nonmigratory species while migratory game bird seasons and bag limits are basically determined within a framework set by federal authorities.

Those wanting to report illegal acts against wildlife should consult their nearest state conservation officer. He is usually to be found in the county seat, often under the state listing in the telephone directory. Or he can be found through the county sheriff's office. The conservation officer will know the wildlife laws and, if need be, can contact the federal game agent who enforces federal wildlife laws.

One common question is whether or not a citizen may keep and nurse back to health an injured bird. This should be checked with the conservation officer. For this, a federal permit is needed for migratory birds. A permit must be obtained from your state or a regional office of the U.S. Bureau of Sport Fisheries and Wildlife. After it recovers, the bird must be released back to the wild.

A Code of Ethics

Birders need to practice good manners in the field both for the welfare of birds and for better human relations. Here are guidelines stressed by the birding community.

Be considerate of other peoples' property. Enter private property only with permission. Consider limiting the size of your group. One or two birders may be more welcome than a crowd of them. Closed gates should be left closed. Take care not to tramp on flowers or cultivated crops. Leave your dog at home.

Be considerate of birds and other wildlife. Be especially careful in nesting seasons not to approach nests too closely. Do not manipulate vegetation to get a better view or camera angle on a nest. Your actions or a change in the appearance of the scene may attract predators. Try to do nothing that will cause the bird to alter its natural behavior. If you discover a nest, move away as quickly and quietly as possible.

The Cincinnati Nature Center offers visitors an excellent opportunity to find woodland species.

Official State Birds

Alabama	Yellow-shafted flicker	Montana	Western meadowlark
Alaska	Willow ptarmigan	Nebraska	Western meadowlark
Arizona	Cactus wren	Nevada	Mountain bluebird
Arkansas	Mockingbird	New Hampshire	Purple finch
California	California quail	New Jersey	American goldfinch
Colorado	Lark bunting	New Mexico	Roadrunner
Connecticut	American robin	New York	Eastern bluebird
Delaware	Blue hen chicken	North Carolina	Cardinal
Florida	Mockingbird	North Dakota	Western meadowlark
Georgia	Brown thrasher	Ohio	Cardinal
Hawaii	Nene goose	Oklahoma	Scissor-tailed flycatcher
Idaho	Mountain bluebird	Oregon	Western meadowlark
Illinois	Cardinal	Pennsylvania	Ruffed grouse
Indiana	Cardinal	Rhode Island	Rhode Island red chicken
Iowa	Goldfinch	South Carolina	Carolina wren
Kansas	Western meadowlark	South Dakota	Ring-necked pheasant
Kentucky	Cardinal	Tennessee	Mockingbird
Louisiana	Brown pelican	Texas	Mockingbird
Maine	Black-capped chickadee	Utah	California gull
Maryland	Baltimore oriole	Vermont	Hermit thrush
Massachusetts	Black-capped chickadee	Virginia	Cardinal
Michigan	American robin	Washington	Goldfinch
Minnesota	Common loon	West Virginia	Cardinal
Mississippi	Mockingbird	Wisconsin	American robin
Missouri	Eastern bluebird	Wyoming	Western meadowlark

Life List

Serious bird watchers are constantly on the alert for a "new" bird, one they have never seen before. When they make a positive identification of such a bird, its name goes onto their own personal life list of birds identified. Year after year this list grows, reflecting the bird watcher's good fortune in finding birds and skill in identifying them. Complete with dates, and perhaps other information of interest, this list becomes the major record of a lifetime of bird watching. The following list of North American birds, arranged for convenient use with modern bird guides, is suggested as a permanent record on which the reader can note dates of his own observations plus other important details.

BIRDS RECORDED BY _____

Name	Date	Notes
Loons		
Common loon		
Yellow-billed loon		
Arctic loon		
Red-throated loon		
Grebes		
Least grebe		
Western grebe		
Red-necked grebe		
Horned grebe		
Eared grebe		
Pied-billed grebe		
Tube Noses		
Laysan albatross		
Black-footed albatross		

	Name	Date	Notes
	Northern fulmar		
	Pink-footed shearwater		
	Cory's shearwater		
	Greater shearwater		
	Flesh-footed shearwater		
	Audubon's shearwater		
	New Zealand shearwater		
	Manx shearwater		
	Sooty shearwater		
	Short-tailed shearwater		
	Slender-billed shearwater		
	Pale-footed shearwater		
	Black-capped petrel		
	Scaled petrel		
	Black storm petrel		
	Ashy storm petrel		
	Fork-tailed storm petrel		
	Leach's storm petrel		
	Wilson's storm petrel		
	Least storm petrel		
	Pelicans and Their Relatives		
	Red-billed tropicbird		
	White-tailed tropicbird		
	Brown pelican		
	White pelican		
	Magnificent frigatebird		
	Northern gannet		
	Masked booby		
	Brown booby		
	Red-footed booby		
	Blue-footed booby		
	Great cormorant		
	Brandt's cormorant		
	Double-crested cormorant		
	Pelagic cormorant		
	Olivaceous cormorant		
	Red-faced cormorant		

Name	Date	Notes
Anhinga		
Waterfowl		
Tundra swan		
Trumpeter swan		
Mute swan		
Brant		
Canada goose		
Barnacle goose		
Emperor goose		
Greater white-fronted goose		
Snow goose		
Ross' goose		
Wood duck		
Mallard		
Mottled duck		
American black duck		
Laysan teal		
Northern pintail		
Gadwall		
American widgeon		
Eurasian widgeon		
Northern shoveler		
Blue-winged teal		
Cinnamon teal		
Green-winged teal		
Baikal teal		
Falcated teal		
Fulvous tree duck		
Black-bellied tree duck		
Canvasback		
Redhead		
Ring-necked duck		
Greater scaup		
Lesser scaup		
Common goldeneye		
Barrow's goldeneye		
Bufflehead		

	Name	Date	Notes
	Common eider		
	King eider		
	Spectacled eider		
	Steller's eider		
	Harlequin duck		
	Oldsquaw		
	Black scoter		
	White-winged scoter		
	Surf scoter		
	Ruddy duck		
	Masked duck		
	Common merganser		
	Hooded merganser		
	Red-breasted merganser		
	Vultures, Hawks, Falcons		
	Turkey vulture		
	Black vulture		
	California condor		
	Osprey		
	White-tailed kite		
	Mississippi kite		
	Black-shouldered kite		
	American swallow-tailed kite		
	Snail kite		
	Northern goshawk		
	Cooper's hawk		
	Sharp-shinned hawk		
	Northern harrier		
	Rough-legged hawk		
	Ferruginous hawk		
	Red-tailed hawk		
	Red-shouldered hawk		
	Swainson's hawk		
	Broad-winged hawk		
	Harris' hawk		
	Black hawk		
	Zone-tailed hawk		

Name	Date	Notes
White-tailed hawk		
Short-tailed hawk		
Gray hawk		
Golden eagle		
Bald eagle		
Crested caracara		
Gyrfalcon		
Prairie falcon		
Peregrine falcon		
Merlin		
American kestrel		
Aplomado falcon		
Gallinaceous Birds		
Wild turkey		
Plain chachalaca		
Blue grouse		
Spruce grouse		
Ruffed grouse		
Sharp-tailed grouse		
Sage grouse		
Greater prairie chicken		
Lesser prairie chicken		
Willow ptarmigan		
Rock ptarmigan		
White-tailed ptarmigan		
Northern bobwhite		
Scaled quail		
California quail		
Gambel's quail		
Mountain quail		
Montezuma quail		
Chukar		
Ring-necked pheasant		
Gray partridge		
Herons and Their Relatives		
Great egret		
Snowy egret		

	Name	Date	Notes
	Cattle egret		
	Great blue heron		
	Reddish egret		
	Little blue heron		
	Tricolored heron		
	Green-backed heron		
	Black-crowned nightheron		
	Yellow-crowned nightheron		
	American bittern		
	Least bittern		
	Jabiru stork		
	Wood stork		
	White-faced ibis		
	Glossy ibis		
	White ibis		
	Scarlet ibis		
	Roseate spoonbill		
	Greater American flamingo		
	Cranes and Their Relatives		
	Sandhill crane		
	Whooping crane		
	Limpkin		
	Virginia rail		
	Sora		
	Black rail		
	Corn crake		
	Yellow rail		
	Clapper rail		
	King rail		
	Common moorhen		
	Purple gallinule		
	American coot		
	Shorebirds, Gulls, Alcids		
	American oystercatcher		
	American black oystercatcher		
	American avocet		
	Black-necked stilt		

	Name	Date	Notes
	Northern lapwing		
	Northern jacana		
	Eurasian dotterel		
	Mountain plover		
	Lesser golden plover		
	Piping plover		
	Black-bellied plover		
	Snowy plover		
	Semipalmated plover		
	Wilson's plover		
	Killdeer		
	Long-billed curlew		
	Bristle-thighed curlew		
	Eskimo curlew		
	Marbled godwit		
	Hudsonian godwit		
	Bar-tailed godwit		
	Upland sandpiper		
	Buff-breasted sandpiper		
	Solitary sandpiper		
	Wood sandpiper		
	Spotted sandpiper		
	Wandering tattler		
	Willet		
	Greater yellowlegs		
	Lesser yellowlegs		
	Stilt sandpaper		
	Short-billed dowitcher		
	Long-billed dowitcher		
	Ruddy turnstone		
	Black turnstone		
	Surfbird		
	Purple sandpiper		
	Rock sandpiper		
	Pectoral sandpiper		
	Knot		
	Ruff		

		Name	Date	Notes
		Curlew sandpiper		
		Dunlin		
		Sanderling		
		White-rumped sandpiper		
		Baird's sandpiper		
		Least sandpiper		
		Semipalmated sandpiper		
		Western sandpiper		
		Wilson's phalarope		
		Red phalarope		
		Red-necked phalarope		
		American woodcock		
		Common snipe		
		Parasitic jaeger		
		Pomarine jaeger		
		Long-tailed jaeger		
		Great skua		
		Laughing gull		
		Franklin's gull		
		Little gull		
		Common black-headed gull		
		Bonaparte's gull		
		Heermann's gull		
		Glaucous gull		
		Glaucous-winged gull		
		Mew gull		
		Ring-billed gull		
		California gull		
		Herring gull		
		Thayer's gull		
		Iceland gull		
		Lesser black-backed gull		
		Western gull		
		Great black-backed gull		
		Ross' gull		
		Sabine's gull		
		Ivory gull		

Name	Date	Notes
Caspian tern		
Gray-backed tern		
Arctic tern		
Common tern		
Roseate tern		
Forster's tern		
Sandwich tern		
Gull-billed tern		
Elegant tern		
Royal tern		
Least tern		
Black tern		
Sooty tern		
Aleutian tern		
Bridled tern		
Brown noddy		
Black noddy		
Black skimmer		
Dovkie		
Razorbill		
Thick-billed murre		
Common murre		
Black guillemot		
Pigeon guillemot		
Atlantic puffin		
Horned puffin		
Tufted puffin		
Crested auklet		
Rhinoceros auklet		
Whiskered auklet		
Cassin's auklet		
Least auklet		
Kittlitz's auklet		
Xantus' murrelet		
Marbled murrelet		
Ancient murrelet		
Parakeet auklet		

	Name	Date	Notes
	Doves and Pigeons		
	Mourning dove		
	Band-tailed pigeon		
	Rock dove		
	White-winged dove		
	White-crowned pigeon		
	Red-billed pigeon		
	Spotted dove		
	Ringed turtle dove		
	Ground dove		
	Inca dove		
	White-fronted dove		
	Ruddy ground dove		
	Cuckoos		
	Mangrove cuckoo		
	Yellow-billed cuckoo		
	Black-billed cuckoo		
	Smooth-billed ani		
	Greater roadrunner		
	Owls		
	Barn owl		
	Eastern screech owl		
	Western screech owl		
	Whiskered screech owl		
	Great horned owl		
	Long-eared owl		
	Short-eared owl		
	Snowy owl		
	Barred owl		
	Spotted owl		
	Great gray owl		
	Northern hawk-owl		
	Burrowing owl		
	Boreal owl		
	Northern saw-whet owl		
	Whiskered owl		
	Flammulated owl		

Name	Date	Notes
Northern pygmy owl		
Ferruginous pigmy owl		
Elf owl		
Goatsuckers		
Common nighthawk		
Lesser nighthawk		
Chuck-will's-widow		
Whip-poor-will		
Poor-will		
Pauraque		
Swifts and Hummingbirds		
Black swift		
Chimney swift		
Vaux's swift		
White-throated swift		
Broad-tailed hummingbird		
Calliope hummingbird		
Anna's hummingbird		
Ruby-throated hummingbird		
Black-chinned hummingbird		
Costa's hummingbird		
Lucifer hummingbird		
Rivoli's hummingbird		
Rufous hummingbird		
Allen's hummingbird		
Blue-throated hummingbird		
Violet-crowned hummingbird		
Buff-bellied hummingbird		
Broad-billed hummingbird		
White-eared hummingbird		
Parrots		
Thick-billed parrot		
Monk parakeet		
Trogons		
Coppery-tailed trogon		
Kingfishers		
Belted kingfisher		

	Name	Date	Notes
	Green kingfisher		
	Ringed kingfisher		
	Woodpeckers		
	Northern flicker		
	Pileated woodpecker		
	Red-bellied woodpecker		
	Golden-fronted woodpecker		
	Gila woodpecker		
	Ladder-backed woodpecker		
	Red-cockaded woodpecker		
	Nuttall's woodpecker		
	Red-headed woodpecker		
	Acorn woodpecker		
	Lewis' woodpecker		
	White-headed woodpecker		
	Yellow-bellied sapsucker		
	Red-breasted sapsucker		
	Williamson's sapsucker		
	Arizona woodpecker		
	Hairy woodpecker		
	Downy woodpecker		
	Strickland's woodpecker		
	Black-backed woodpecker		
	Three-toed woodpecker		
	Perching Birds		
	Rose-throated becard		
	Scissor-tailed flycatcher		
	Great kiskadee		
	Vermilion flycatcher		
	Sulphur-bellied flycatcher		
	Eastern kingbird		
	Western kingbird		
	Cassin's kingbird		
	Tropical kingbird		
	Gray kingbird		
	Thick-billed kingbird		
	Great crested flycatcher		

Name	Date	Notes
Wied's crested flycatcher		
Ash-throated flycatcher		
Olivaceous flycatcher		
Eastern phoebe		
Black phoebe		
Say's phoebe		
Yellow-bellied flycatcher		
Acadian flycatcher		
Alder flycatcher		
Willow flycatcher		
Least flycatcher		
Hammond's flycatcher		
Dusky flycatcher		
Gray flycatcher		
Western flycatcher		
Buff-breasted flycatcher		
Beardless flycatcher		
Greater pewee		
Eastern wood pewee		
Western wood pewee		
Olive-sided flycatcher		
Horned lark		
Violet-green swallow		
Tree swallow		
Barn swallow		
Cliff swallow		
Cave swallow		
Bank swallow		
Northern rough-winged swallow		
Purple martin		
Scrub jay		
Gray-breasted jay		
Pinyon jay		
Blue jay		
Steller's jay		
Gray jay		
Green jay		

	Name	Date	Notes
	Black-billed magpie		
	Yellow-billed magpie		
	Clark's nutcracker		
	Common raven		
	Chiuhuahuan raven		
	American crow		
	Northwestern crow		
	Fish crow		
	Black-capped chickadee		
	Carolina chickadee		
	Mountain chickadee		
	Mexican chickadee		
	Boreal chickadee		
	Chestnut-backed chickadee		
	Tufted titmouse		
	Plain titmouse		
	Bridled titmouse		
	Verdin		
	Common bushtit		
	Wrentit		
	Red-whiskered bulbul		
	American dipper		
	White-breasted nuthatch		
	Red-breasted nuthatch		
	Brown-headed nuthatch		
	Pygmy nuthatch		
	Brown creeper		
	House wren		
	Winter wren		
	Bewick's wren		
	Carolina wren		
	Cactus wren		
	Marsh wren		
	Sedge wren		
	Rock wren		
	Canyon wren		
	Northern mockingbird		

Name	Date	Notes
Gray catbird		
Sage thrasher		
Brown thrasher		
Long-billed thrasher		
Bendire's thrasher		
Curve-billed thrasher		
California thrasher		
Crissal thrasher		
Le Conte's thrasher		
American robin		
Vried thrush		
Townsend's solitaire		
Bluethroat		
Northern wheatear		
Wood thrush		
Hermit thrush		
Veery		
Swainson's thrush		
Gray-cheeked thrush		
Eastern bluebird		
Western bluebird		
Mountain bluebird		
Blue-gray gnatcatcher		
Black-tailed gnatcatcher		
Ruby-crowned kinglet		
Golden-crowned kinglet		
Arctic warbler		
Water pipit		
Sprague's pipit		
White wagtail		
Yellow wagtail		
Bohemian waxwing		
Cedar waxwing		
Phainopepla		
Northern shrike		
Loggerhead shrike		
European starling		

	Name	Date	Notes
	Crested myna		
	Blacked-capped vireo		
	Gray vireo		
	Solitary vireo		
	Red-eyed vireo		
	White-eyed vireo		
	Bell's vireo		
	Hutton's vireo		
	Yellow-throated vireo		
	Black-whiskered vireo		
	Yellow-green vireo		
	Philadelphia vireo		
	Warbling vireo		
	Black-and-white warbler		
	Black-throated blue warbler		
	Cerulean warbler		
	Black-throated green warbler		
	Black-throated gray warbler		
	Prothonotary warbler		
	Swainson's warbler		
	Worm-eating warbler		
	Golden-winged warbler		
	Blue-winged warbler		
	Backman's warbler		
	Tennessee warbler		
	Orange-crowned warbler		
	Nashville warbler		
	Olive warbler		
	Olive-backed warbler		
	Virginia's warbler		
	Colima warbler		
	Lucy's warbler		
	Parula warbler		
	Yellow warbler		
	Magnolia warbler		
	Cape May warbler		
	Yellow-rumped warbler		

Name	Date	Notes
Townsend's warbler		
Golden-cheeked warbler		
Hermit warbler		
Yellow-throated warbler		
Grace's warbler		
Blackburnian warbler		
Chestnut-sided warbler		
Blackpoll warbler		
Pine warbler		
Kirtland's warbler		
Prairie warbler		
Bay-breasted warbler		
Palm warbler		
Northern waterthrush		
Louisiana waterthrush		
Ovenbird		
Yellowthroat		
Yellow-breasted chat		
Kentucky warbler		
MacGillivray's warbler		
Mourning warbler		
Connecticut warbler		
Hooded warbler		
Red-faced warbler		
Wilson's warbler		
Canada warbler		
American redstart		
Painted redstart		
House sparrow		
Eurasian tree sparrow		
Western tanager		
Scarlet tanager		
Summer tanager		
Hepatic tanager		
Blue-gray tanager		
Bobolink		
Eastern meadowlark		

	Name	Date	Notes
	Western meadowlark		
	Yellow-headed blackbird		
	Red-winged blackbird		
	Rusty blackbird		
	Tricolored blackbird		
	Brewer's blackbird		
	Boat-tailed grackle		
	Great-tailed grackle		
	Common grackle		
	Brown-headed cowbird		
	Bronzed cowbird		
	Orchard oriole		
	Black-headed oriole		
	Scott's oriole		
	Hooded oriole		
	Baltimore oriole		
	Bullock's oriole		
	Altamira oriole		
	Spotted-breasted oriole		
	Streaked-backed oriole		
	Cardinal		
	Pyrrhuloxia		
	Evening grosbeak		
	Rose-breasted grosbeak		
	Black-headed grosbeak		
	Blue grosbeak		
	Indigo bunting		
	Lazuli bunting		
	Varied bunting		
	Painted bunting		
	House finch		
	Purple finch		
	Cassin's finch		
	Gray-crowned rosy finch		
	Black rosy finch		
	Brown-capped rosy finch		
	Hoary redpoll		

	Name	Date	Notes
	Common redpoll		
	Pine siskin		
	American goldfinch		
	Lesser goldfinch		
	Lawrence's goldfinch		
	European goldfinch		
	Red crossbill		
	Pine grosbeak		
	White-winged crossbill		
	White-collared seedeater		
	Green-tailed towhee		
	Rufous-sided towhee		
	Brown towhee		
	Abert's towhee		
	Bachman's sparrow		
	Olive sparrow		
	Savannah sparrow		
	Grasshopper sparrow		
	Baird's sparrow		
	Henslow's sparrow		
	Le Conte's sparrow		
	Sharp-tailed sparrow		
	Seaside sparrow		
	Vesper sparrow		
	Lark sparrow		
	Black-throated sparrow		
	Sage sparrow		
	Dark-eyed junco		
	Yellow-eyed junco		
	Rufous-winged sparrow		
	Rufous-crowned sparrow		
	Cassin's sparrow		
	Botteri's sparrow		
	Tree sparrow		
	Chipping sparrow		
	Clay-colored sparrow		
	Brewer's sparrow		

	Name	Date	Notes
	Field sparrow		
	Black-chinned sparrow		
	Harris' sparrow		
	White-crowned sparrow		
	Golden-crowned sparrow		
	White-throated sparrow		
	Fox sparrow		
	Lincoln's sparrow		
	Swamp sparrow		
	Song sparrow		
	McCown's longspur		
	Lapland longspur		
	Chestnut-collared longspur		
	Smith's longspur		
	Snow bunting		
	McKay's bunting		
	Lark bunting		
	Dickcissel		